LET THEM EAT KETCHUP!

LET THEM EAT KETCHUP!

The Politics of Poverty and Inequality

SHEILA COLLINS

MONTHLY REVIEW PRESS
NEW YORK

Library of Congress Cataloging-in-Publication Data

Collins, Sheila D.
   Let them eat ketchup! : the politics of poverty and inequality / by Sheila D.
Collins.
      p.   cm. — (Cornerstone books)
   Includes bibliographical references and index.
   ISBN 0-85345-904-5 : $24.00 — ISBN 0-85345-905-3 (pbk.) : $12.00
   1. Poverty. 2. Poor. I. Title. II. Series: Cornerstone books (New York, N.Y.)
HC79.P6C63 1995
362.5′8—dc20   94-31724
                                                                      CIP

Monthly Review Press
122 West 27th Street
New York, NY 10001

Manufactured in the United States of America
10 9 8 7 6 5 4 3 2 1

CONTENTS

ACKNOWLEDGEMENTS

My initial interest in poverty as a function of politics was ignited by the ten-year in-your-face education I got in the subject while living and working in East Harlem (New York City) during the critical years of President Johnson's War on Poverty. I am forever grateful to my husband, John, for sharing those tumultuous years with me.

I came to know some of poverty's other faces in the late 1970s and early 1980s, when I worked for United Methodist Voluntary Service, a program providing small grants and technical support to poor people's organizations across the country. To people like Ron Chisom, Barbara Major, Diana Dunn, Anne Braden, Diana Ortiz, Arnette Lewis, and the late Jim Dunn, among others, I owe a deep debt of thanks for an incomparable education in how the systems of oppression feed each other and operate to thwart human potential and democratic possibility. From them, I also learned how the poor can and do continually resist their oppression.

My colleagues in New Initiatives for Full Employment and the National Jobs for All Coalition have helped me to combine experience with rigorous academic analysis, theory with action. I am particularly grateful to Trudy Goldberg, Helen Ginsburg, Sumner Rosen, and June Zaccone for turning me on to research I might not have known about and for the intellectual stimulation and critique that has been so valuable a part of my growth over the last eight years.

Finally, I would like to thank Susan Lowes, Director of Monthly Review Press, for making this opportunity possible, and my editor, Ethan Young, for helping to turn my turgid academic prose into ordinary language.

1

CLASS AND POVERTY: MYTHS AND REALITIES

President Bill Clinton came into office claiming to be a "new kind of Democrat," who would address the needs of an embattled middle class. Before him, President Ronald Reagan said he spoke for "middle America"; in 1972 President Richard Nixon posed as the champion of what he called the "silent majority"— the "man in the middle."

President George Bush once asserted that class "is for European democracies or something else—it isn't for the United States. We are not going to be divided by class."[1] From sitcoms to the local classroom, we have grown used to thinking of the United States as a classless society. While it is sometimes acknowledged that some are "rich" and others "poor," most of us, most of the time, think of ourselves as belonging to one big, comfortable middle class. A popular U.S. government college text reinforces this image when it declares: "Economic resources are better distributed in America than in most other societies today. Most Americans are in the middle class. . . . "[2] Even in the midst of the Great Depression, when the unemployment rate soared to over 20 percent, eight out of ten Americans claimed to be middle class.[3]

What do we mean by "middle class?" And how do we know we are in it?

I grew up in the 1950s in a middle-sized northeastern city in an all-white neighborhood of small homes. We owned our own home (or rather, the bank did) and we had a car (also owned by the bank) which had to last us for a lifetime. My father and my friends' fathers all had jobs, while our mothers, for the most part, were housewives. In the postwar years we were enjoying the American Dream: a house, a car, and "a chicken in every pot"—at least on Sundays. Those I grew up with—whose fathers (many of them World War II veterans) were painters, printers, plumbers, carpenters, and machine tool operators—took for granted that they were part of the great American middle class. For most, I suspect, being middle class meant having the promise of continuous upward mobility—at least having the chance, if not to attend college yourself, to be able to send your son to college so that he could move beyond a life of manual labor. (In those days, when you had money for only one college education, it was usually assumed it would go to the son!)

Yet beneath the surface of this glorified Dream lurked a more sobering reality. The death of a father or the chronic illness of a member of the family could easily wipe out whatever equity was in that house or car. My father, whose job as a commercial artist was a bit less secure than the jobs held by my friends' fathers, never got out from under the constant worry about where the next paycheck was coming from. He died of a heart attack at the age of fifty-two, having taken only a single five-day vacation in his entire working life. I was one of only two of my childhood friends to go on to college—and only because I got a large enough scholarship. My girl friends graduated from high school and got jobs as secretaries and bookkeepers, while their boyfriends followed their fathers into the skilled crafts or joined the army or police force.

On the south side of town—literally on the "other side of the tracks"—was a community that was far less comfortable than ours. There, people mostly rented run-down apartments and traveled by public transportation (if they had cars, they were ancient). If they didn't live on welfare grants, they worked as maids in the large homes of the corporate executives that sat on acres of artfully landscaped lawns in the north end of the city, or worked from early morning to late at night in their own small businesses, catering to the almost completely isolated community residents. Almost none of their children expected to go to college.

The existence of this community (overwhelmingly black) as well as the existence of the (completely white) community that lived in comparative splendor to the north, was completely unknown to my friends and me until we were all brought together in the city's only high school. All of us—the children of corporate executives, machine tool operators, and maids—thought of ourselves as middle class.

THE MIDDLE MUDDLE

It is typical of the mental gimcrackery that passes for a public philosophy these days that our rulers are suddenly frantic to grant boons to the middle class. And what is it, this middle class, which all statesmen from President to Congressional doorkeeper now yearn to pelt with blessings?... It is an abstraction, a fragment of a campaign slogan, a piety on a demagogue's tongue, an insoluble calculus problem for demographers, a verbal crutch for economists and political writers required by the cruel nature of their trades to sound eloquent while waiting for an idea to pull into the station.—*Russell Baker*[4]

The idea that our society is composed of one big middle class has been used to sell everything from life insurance to presidents. But it is a myth—a fiction that energizes our national ideals while obscuring the real differences in income, wealth, and power that exist in the United States. Yet millions of immigrants each year leave families and risk lives to get here. For them, the myth is the stuff of their most heartfelt dreams. Since conditions in many developing or war-torn countries are so much worse, most immigrants are able to do better here than they did at home. But for everyone, sooner or later, dream clashes with life in a moment of truth.

CLASS: THE GREAT TABOO

The truth is that the United States is a deeply divided society. The movements that erupted over the last thirty years exposed the unacknowledged (but ever-present) fault lines of color, gender, and sexual orientation. But there is another source of division that cross-cuts all of these—that of class.

The concept of "class" is used by sociologists and economists to describe differences between people that are based on economic position—income and wealth, occupational group, etc. Class differences imply differences in power. Yet one rarely hears the term mentioned in this country except in relation to the *middle class*. In fact, some have called *class* the most taboo subject in the United States. This is not so in Europe or in many other parts of the world, where the reality of class is openly acknowledged and political parties and campaigns are forged around class interests. For example, if my parents had lived in England, they would have belonged to the Labor Party. In Italy, they might have voted for the Communist Party, which in that country claimed a huge base among ordinary workers during the post-World War II era. Instead, they considered it natural to back the Democratic Party, which can claim the loyalty of organized labor along with that of super-rich and powerful corporate types.

It should be obvious that differences in income and wealth go a long way in determining our life chances: where we live; how much we have to spend on luxuries; the kind of health care and education we receive; the amount of leisure we can enjoy; the amount of control we have over our work; and what kind of recognition we can expect from public officials. People here, like everywhere, are grouped in society by all these factors, as well as by how we survive—whether on wages, salaries, or access to accumulated wealth. We all take our place in society as part of one or another class, know it or not, like it or not.

The government's own statistics on income distribution say a lot about the nature of class inequality. Each year, the Census Bureau surveys a representative sample of 60,000 households, both families and individuals, asking them questions about their pre-tax incomes.[5] From this sample all kinds of information are derived, such as the gender, racial, age, and geographical distribution of income, the sizes of families dependent on certain levels of income, and so on. The government currently includes as income not only wages and salaries, but money from dividends, interest, royalties, net rental income, Social Security, welfare payments, pensions, and such other miscellaneous sources as alimony. It excludes such sources as inheritances, gifts, capital gains or losses, the value of fringe benefits, in-kind income such as free meals, or the value of government transfer payments such as food stamps or Medicaid/Medicare.

There are two ways that the Census Bureau measures the distribution of income, and therefore income inequality. The first is by ranking all households (or families) from lowest to highest on the basis of income and then dividing the population into equal groups, called *quintiles*, each representing 20 percent of the total.[6] The aggregate income of each group is then divided by the overall income to determine each quintile's share. This picture of income shares gives us a fairly adequate (though not completely accurate) measure of income inequality in the United States.[7]

The second method of measuring income inequality involves incorporating more detailed income data into a single statistic, called the *Gini index*. This statistic summarizes how all income shares are dispersed across society's whole income distribution, using a standard of total equality as its measure. The Gini index ranges from zero (perfect equality), where the total income is shared equally by everyone, to one, which indicates perfect *in*equality—where all the income is received by only one recipient. The Gini index is normally neither zero nor one, but somewhere in between. In 1993 the measurement for the nation's households was .447.[8] This index is most useful in measuring long-term changes in income inequality and in comparing inequality across geographical boundaries. Both these ways of measuring inequality provide important information about the structure of U.S. society and the relative amounts of power held by various groups.

Figure 1-1
Shares of Total Income Received
by Household Income Groups
(by percent)

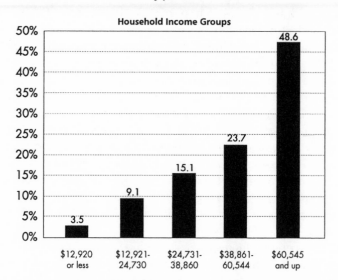

Source: U.S. Bureau of the Census, *Current Population Reports,*
Series pp. 60-188, *Income, Poverty, and Valuation of Noncash Benefits: 1993*
(Washington, D.C.: U.S. Government Printing Office, 1995), Figure 1, p.xii

Figure 1-1 illustrates how lopsided income distribution in the United States is. The top 20 percent of households receive almost half of all the nation's household income, while the bottom 20 percent receive a minuscule 3.5 percent! What's more, the top 5 percent of the population ($99,372 income and up) receives over five times the share of the bottom 20 percent.

Take another look at Figure 1-1. Which portion represents the middle class? Is it the third quintile? Or is it all three of the middle columns? It depends on how "middle class" is defined.

Statisticians working with measures of income have used figures with ranges as wide as $55,000 between the lower and upper cutoff points. During the 1992 campaign, President Clinton's estimate of the middle class included families with incomes between $20,000 and $65,000.[9] Economist Frederick Strobel, who has written about the decline of the middle class, defines it as essentially "a labor-dependent group if currently working or, if retired, a transfer-dependent group, that is, living off Social Security and pension incomes" (as opposed to the rich, who, if their incomes were to stop, could still live comfortably off their stocks, bonds, and other financial assets).[10] According to Clinton and Strobel, the middle class consists of everyone who must work for a living, including those who go home at night to a spacious suburban home equipped with three television sets, a VCR, and a CD player, as well as those who can't even afford a telephone!

In 1994 the Republicans used an even more elastic definition. They proposed a tax credit for a "middle class" that included families making as much as $250,000 a year.

Knowing what the highest and lowest cutoff points in each quintile are might help us to understand more about the purchasing power of each group. But before reading further, look at Figure 1-1 again and attempt to place your own household income in one of these quintiles. Where are you—exactly in the middle, or toward one end or the other?

A large percentage of our population is economically vulnerable. We know from the Census Bureau that in 1992 households with incomes between $25,000 and $100,000 had an average of 1.92 earners. If just *one* of the earners in a four-person household with a combined income of $45,000 was to lose his or her job, the household or family could be thrown into poverty. For example, a national poll taken by the Gallup Organization in 1988 asked how much money was needed by a family of four "just to get along." The average answer was $20,913.[11] Adjusting this for inflation brings the figure to $24,802 in 1992.

MIDDLE CLASS AND SHELLSHOCKED

Like a mantra said daily over the shambles of his life, Marvin Pedowitz repeats: "I'm not going to lose my cool. I am in control." ...For Mr. Pedowitz, a 39-year-old accountant, and tens of thousands of other solidly middle-class men and women thrown out of work by a weak economy, the recession has gone on too long. The effort to maintain a sense of control over their lives, emotions and dignity has become a daily challenge....

Walking into a welfare office is confirmation of their fear that they have hit bottom. "They are a completely shellshocked group," said Nancy Glass, commissioner of the Westchester County Social Services Department, which has recorded an 18 percent increase in welfare cases since 1990....

"I live in a completely different America today than I did two or three years ago," said Mr. Pedowitz, who has been out of full-time work since 1990, has fallen behind on his child-support payments, has no home of his own and stays ahead of bill collectors by living with friends in New Jersey whom he repays by doing their tax returns....

"I was raised to think that if you got an education, acquired skills and made sound investments, you would always have a job and money in the bank," he said, looking shattered as he recalled the suddenness of his fall from suburban grace.—*New York Times*[12]

Combining households that make $65,500 with the country's highest earners in the top quintile hides more than a simple income gap. Families and households making $65,500 in 1993 may have been fairly comfortable as long as their main earners were bringing in money; but few of them had much of a cushion beyond their houses and cars in the event their incomes were reduced or disappeared or they incurred extraordinary expenses for something like catastrophic illness. On the other hand, within this same quintile in 1992 were Stephen J. Ross and N.J. Nicholas, Jr., then co-chief executives of Time Warner, who together made $99.6 million. Those at their level could easily lose a few million on the stock market or suffer a catastrophic illness and still be millionaires.[13]

A picture of the income distribution of the U.S. population is so lopsided as we reach the top 1 percent that it is not possible to draw the proportions on a sheet of paper this size. If we were to graph all of the income in the country and make one-sixteenth of an inch represent income increments of one thousand dollars, we would have to have a graph that stretched up over 390 feet to accommodate the highest income earners! In other words, the gap between the richest and the poorest *within* the top fifth of income earners ($99,372 and up) is far greater than the gap between the bottom layer of the top fifth and the bottom layer of the bottom fifth!

AT THE TOP OF THE HEAP

America's corporate executives shrugged off the onus of slipping profits as their paychecks climbed to new highs in 1991.... At the top of the heap was Anthony J.F. O'Reilly, the head boss at H.J. Heinz Co., who pulled in $75 million. His average weekly income of $1,442,307.59 was 4,000 times more than the pay of the average U.S. worker, who earned $354.66 a week before taxes.
As the board chairman and chief executive officer of Heinz, O'Reilly

was among the hundreds of corporate bosses who collected extrava-
gant pay envelopes last year despite the lingering recession, overall
sluggish company performance and mass layoffs.

The CEOs of blue-chip companies pocketed an average of $2.5 mil-
lion each with their salaries, bonuses and stock awards for an
increase of 26 percent over their 1990 compensation level, according to a Business Week survey. Of the 800 chief executives covered
by a Forbes magazine survey, the average compensation was $1 mil-
lion in 1991.

But on the shop floor, the average working stiff earned about
$18,542 in 1991, an increase of 2.6 percent over the year, accord-
ing to the Bureau of Labor Statistics.—*AFL-CIO News*[14]

GENDER, RACE, AND EDUCATIONAL BACKGROUND

As bad as the general income gap appears, the income shares
by gender, race, and educational level are worse. In 1993, median
income for females ($11,046) was a little over half that for males
($21,102), and the income of black males ($14,605) was only 66
percent that of white males ($21,981). The gap between white and
black females was less—about 16 percentage points—a little over
half the gap that existed between white and black male earnings.[15]

Is education the ticket to equal opportunity and greater prosperity, as so many seem to think? Millions are now entering
college or going back to school on the assumption that their
college or graduate school credentials will translate into significantly higher incomes. Clinton administration Labor Secretary
Robert Reich has made education and training the cornerstones
of his labor policy. Yet although educational attainment and
income are closely related for white males, things are different
for other groups, particularly women, African-Americans, and
Latinos.

According to census statistics, female college graduates made
only 60 percent of what males with the same credentials made
and a little more than 1 percentage point above what male high

school graduates made. Females with master's degrees did only slightly better. However, females with professional degrees made only 58 percent of what males with professional degrees made, while females with doctorates made only 66 percent of the earnings of males with doctorates. Black male college graduates made only 73 percent compared to their white male peers. Black males with master's degrees still trailed with 87 percent. (The numbers of blacks and Hispanics with graduate degrees were considered too small for comparative analysis.)[16]

Although white and black females were much closer in earnings than their male counterparts, with black female college graduates actually surpassing the earnings of white female college graduates, this does not necessarily mean that black females were actually earning more. Rather, it may mean that more white women with college degrees were able to drop out of the workforce or take part-time jobs because their husbands earned more than the husbands of black women.

Asian-Americans are celebrated by some (usually white) sociologists as a group that excels in higher education and the professions. But according to the census bureau their median salaries continue to lag behind, although statistically Asian-Americans complete more years of school than do whites. Asian-American high school graduates earned 79 percent of what their white counterparts made, while Asian-American male college graduates made only 90 percent of the median salary of white men. The salaries of Asian-American and white women were more nearly equal to each other's.[17]

In those situations where racial and gender discrimination in the workplace are challenged by education, discrimination keeps winning. Why?

WEALTH AND INEQUALITY

Income levels alone don't tell the whole story about inequality. Wealth is also important, not only because it provides financial stability in the face of sudden loss of income, but because it enables those who hold it to get richer and to control the labor and credit of others. Wealth offers access to enormous political power.

"Them that's got shall get, them that's not shall lose" sang Billie Holiday. Wealth, as both security and power, takes a number of forms held by various groups in our society. Wealth consists of assets that, although not available immediately as money, could be turned into money. People with similar incomes in any given year could have very different levels of wealth, because most wealth is either inherited or accumulated over a lifetime—although those with more income do tend to have more wealth as well.

Most Americans with assets have them invested in such consumer durables as homes and cars. Among the truly rich, however, types of assets change dramatically from physical items to paper assets—mainly stocks and bonds.[18]

In 1989, 89 percent of the financial assets in the country—the type of wealth that generates more income—was held by the richest 10 percent, while the bottom 90 percent of the population held only about 10.6 percent. For all the cheerleading in government and media for entrepreneurial spirit and small business, business ownership figures show that the wealthiest 1 percent owned *over half of all business assets*, while the great majority (90 percent) owned only 18.8 percent![19]

According to researchers at the Federal Reserve Board and the Internal Revenue Service, in 1989 the top 1 percent of households was worth more than the bottom 90 percent. The richest 1 percent commanded 38.3 percent of total net worth (all assets, including real estate, stocks and bonds, checking and savings accounts, etc., minus debts), while the richest 10 percent commanded almost 70 percent of the country's net worth. The remaining 90 percent owned only a little over 30 percent of total net worth![20]

Based on these and earlier findings, researchers Lawrence Mishel and Jared Bernstein speculate that more than half of all U.S. families are living from paycheck to paycheck with little or nothing in the bank in case of a serious financial emergency.[21]

According to a special 1988 Census Bureau study, white households had ten times the net worth of black households—$43,279 for whites, $4,169 for blacks—and almost eight times the net worth of Hispanic households ($5,520).[22] In the same survey, 29 percent of blacks reported having no wealth at all; by contrast, only 8.7 percent of all white households and 24 percent of Hispanic households reported no wealth.[23]

Over twice the proportion of whites as blacks owned income-generating securities (real estate, stocks, bonds, and trusts), while blacks were eight times more likely to get some or all of their income from public assistance (welfare) as whites.[24] While African-Americans make up 12.5 percent of the population, they owned only 3.1 percent of the nation's businesses in 1987. Only 17 percent of those firms had any paid employees—compared with 25 percent of all U.S. firms. African-American firms had only half the level of capitalization of all U.S. firms and accounted for only 1 percent of sales/receipts.[25]

Moreover, African-Americans owned only 0.5 percent of the number and 0.06 percent of the assets of all banks, savings and loan institutions, and insurance companies.[26] The lack of black-owned credit institutions is a major reason for the overall poverty within the black community, as well as its lack of political power—since blacks have historically faced discrimination from white-owned credit institutions.

TRENDS IN INEQUALITY

Even though people in the United States are not locked by birth into their class positions, great inequality has been a constant feature of life. In the country's founding days, a small elite of white male doctors, merchants, bankers, lawyers, and slaveholders wrote a constitution that excluded the vast majority of the population from its protections.

This majority included all women, indigenous peoples, African slaves, and all men without property. One historian concluded that "the wealth inequalities in the thirteen colonies were

about on a par with those in the United States nearly two hundred years later."[27]

While the disparities have remained in place, there was a
move toward greater equality beginning in the 1950s and continuing through the 1960s, when a unique spurt of economic growth
coupled with low inflation was followed by President Johnson's
"War on Poverty." However, that period was to be short-lived.
By the early 1970s, the Gini index had begun to move up again,
and in the 1980s it accelerated its upward pace. Between 1967
and 1993, the Gini index moved closer to perfect inequality by
about 15 percent, erasing whatever gains had been made in
reducing inequality in the previous decades.

Increasing inequality returned with a vengeance, driven by
changes in both the general economy and government policy.
For the average worker, this meant more permanent unemployment and underemployment—the result of changes in the structure of the labor market rather than the usual cause, cyclical ups
and downs in the economy. For those who still had a job, it meant
declining *real* (inflation-adjusted) wages.

The Census Bureau reported in 1994, for example, that the
percentage of all Americans who work full-time but earn less
than the poverty level for a family of four rose by 50 percent in
thirteen years, and this trend has affected every group in our
society.[28] People who work in the same field and are of similar
age and education, regardless of race or gender, are finding that
their wages, once very close, are now spread over a much wider
range. "Inequality is going up in nearly every occupation,"
according to Lawrence Katz, a Harvard labor economist. For
example, in 1980 young lawyers just starting out in the field of
pension law could expect to earn similar salaries. By 1990, the
wage spread for such a position was as large as $68,000. Before,
people could expect to receive roughly the same pay if they
switched jobs—but not any more.[29]

The very rich, on the other hand, saw their incomes skyrocket
during this time. According to the Internal Revenue Service,
from 1980 to 1990 incomes for those making over $1 million a

year increased by 2,184 percent, while incomes for those making $200,000 to $1 million increased by 697 percent.[30]

Some writers have identified a decline of the middle class. The Census Bureau found that between 1968 and 1993, the top fifth of the population gained 5.4 percent of total income, the middle three fifths lost 4.8 percent, and the bottom fifth lost 0.6 percent. But within the top fifth, however, more than half of the gains (almost 60 percent) went to the top 5 percent.[31] Even more startling changes appeared in pre- and post-tax incomes between 1977 and 1989 based on tax returns. More than two thirds of the growth in average pretax incomes went to the wealthiest 1 percent of families. After-tax income inequality was slightly reduced: the super-rich gained a mere 60 percent of the total growth.[32]

The wealth of the affluent (largely in stocks and bonds) rose in the 1980s to what one economist labeled "Great Gatsby levels," that is, from merely well-to-do to spectacular.[33] By 1989 all of that increase in wealth had gone to those at the very top of the heap.[34]

SUMMERTIME AND THE LIVIN' IS EASY

Hardly anyone carries a suitcase. They don't need to. Most have stunning houses stuffed to the gills with everything they need for a Hamptons weekend.... By train, plane, helicopter, bus and car, the financial world's billionaires and mere millionaires flock to the southern fork of the east end of Long Island like European royalty heading for St. Tropez on the French Riviera.... It has everything the average plutocrat needs: World-class beaches maintained by the federal government. A temperate climate. A large inventory of palatial houses and swank private clubs. Few criminals, aside from a few Wall Streeters.... If you've got $3 million to spare on a weekend house, you too could join the happy fray.... This summer a financier rented a prime oceanfront estate for the period from Memorial Day through Labor Day for $350,000....—*Washington Post* [35]

"Modern Horatio Algers notwithstanding, a wave of recent studies shows that rags-to-riches remains the exception, not the rule," the *New York Times* reported. If anything, the climb out of poverty has become more difficult, especially for the young, the unskilled, and the undereducated. According to economist Gary Solon, a child whose father is in the bottom 5 percent of earners has only one chance in twenty of making it into the top 20 percent of families. The same child has a one-in-four chance of rising above the median wealth and a two-in-five chance of staying poor or near poor.[36]

While some may take one step up or one step back, precious few fall from or rise to great heights. Lady Day's economic analysis still applies: "God blessed the child that's got his own."

Even as four-fifths of all Americans saw both their incomes and their wealth decline during the 1980s and early 1990s, African-Americans as a whole (with the exception of a small group of athletes, movie stars, and CEOs) experienced a deeper downward turn than whites. Job status for young African-American males fell relative to whites–even within the same industry and with the same educational levels and work experience.[37] This was contrary to the period between 1967 and 1991, when African-Americans had begun to move modestly toward greater parity. The height of that modest gain was reached in 1988, when per capita black income measured 59.5 percent of per capita white income. Since then, the gap has widened.

What's more, increasing numbers of African-Americans have been reduced to poverty (33.1 percent in 1993) and permanent unemployment. For African-Americans, the Urban League has reported, "the entire period has been characterized by conditions that would be considered depression level if they were experienced by all Americans."[38] Census results show that conditions are especially desperate for young African-Americans, who may be just starting out to raise families.[39]

Although this decline in both absolute and relative status has taken place in a period of moderate economic expansion, there has been no effort to make social programs help those caught in the downward spiral. In fact, as we will see in Chapters 4 and 5, such programs have been steadily reduced or eliminated.

During the same years, the proportion of whites living in poverty declined from 12.8 percent to 12.2 percent.[40] That trend, however, did not hold for the very young, white *or* black. After a period of decreasing poverty in the late 1960s, the poverty rate for children began to climb again in 1974 and is back at roughly the level it was at in 1963.

On paper, there has been more parity between male and female incomes since the 1960s. Median income for females in 1967 was 32.4 percent of males', and in 1993 it was 52 percent. The closing of this gap in the earlier years can be traced to women's entry into previously male-dominated fields, as well as enforcement of anti-discrimination laws. But most of the gains since 1980 are due to declines in real male wages, rather than to any improvements in the workplace for women!

THE MYTH OF CLASSLESSNESS

Far from being one big classless society, the United States is a nation of stark contrasts. Deep and unrelenting economic deprivation and humiliation coexist with wealth that would make the kings and queens of old look like middle-class shopowners. During the Reagan, Bush, and Clinton years, under the guise of carrying out their promise to cut taxes for the middle class, congressional Republicans and Democrats have presided over one of history's largest transfers of wealth to the already wealthy.

Yet the myth of a classless United States persists, even as so many admire and aspire to "lifestyles of the rich and famous." This social schizophrenia—a constant state of confusion between fantasy and reality—may be the only way to make "common sense" of the blatantly unfair and destructive situation that confronts everyone on a daily basis.

The logic of the myth of classlessness—of unlimited upward mobility for anyone who is willing to work for it—reinforces the belief that our economic system distributes its rewards according to merit. Those who don't succeed, it is constantly explained, haven't made the effort, or are by character or by genetic makeup incapable of making it. In other words, failure is the fault of the individual. During times of widespread economic distress, such as depressions and recessions, the cause of such failures is often shifted to "outside" forces, such as oil crises, natural disasters, or "government interference."[41]

But not only is upward mobility a mirage for the majority, its promise blurs some hard realities. In fact, as Chapter 3 explains, capitalism *needs* inequality in order to function and continuously reproduces inequalities as part of its normal operation.

The myth serves the system in several ways. It offers an incentive to work harder—often in jobs that are dull, repetitive, and economically unrewarding—in the hopes of achieving the ever-elusive American Dream. And it pits the lure of individual success against a range of options involving collective action. In short, it is a form of social control.

Economic power and political power are intricately linked. However much we pride ourselves on our political democracy, those with the most wealth ultimately have the most to say about politics most of the time—especially about those policies that affect economic life. The poorest are, for all intents and purposes, disenfranchised. Bernie Sanders of Vermont, the only member of Congress to be elected as an independent on a specifically pro-working class platform, has described the U.S. political system as an *oligarchy* (rule by a few).

> Oligarchy refers not just to the unfair distribution of wealth, but to the fact that the *decisions* that shape our consciousness and affect our lives are made by a very small and powerful group of people.... The mass media (television, radio, newspapers, magazines, publishers, movie and video companies), for example, are largely controlled by a few multi-national corporations that determine the news and programming we see, hear and read—and, ultimately, what we believe. While violence, scandal, horror, sports, and Rush Limbaugh are given much attention, we are provided with virtually no in-depth analysis of the problems facing working people,

or their possible solutions.... Economic decisions that wreck the lives of millions of American families are made by a handful of CEOs. While these corporate leaders bemoan the breakdown of "morality" and "law and order," they close down profitable companies, cut wages and benefits, deny retired workers their pensions and transport our jobs to Third World countries. American workers, who have often given decades of their lives to these companies, have absolutely no say as to what happens to them on the job. They are powerless and expendable, which is what oligarchy is all about.[42]

Politicians, who owe their political careers either to their own fortunes or to others with big money, get the rest of us to vote for them by promising to reduce taxes for the middle class, or to get tough on "welfare cheats," criminals, and other outsiders. They present themselves as ordinary people who rose out of the middle class through talent and hard work, living proof that anyone can make it to the top.

Yet historically, when the political rhetoric says "one big happy family," the strategies and tactics call for cynical manipulation of feelings of powerlessness, economic insecurity, and loss of status—feelings that are part of living in a class system.

CLASS STRUGGLE, USA

In framing a system which we wish to last for ages, we should not lose sight of the changes which ages will produce. An increase of population will of necessity increase the proportion of those who will labor under all the hardships of life, and secretly sigh for a more equal distribution of its blessings. These may in time outnumber those who are placed above the feelings of indigence. According to the equal laws of suffrage, the power will slide into the hands of the former.... How is this danger to be guarded against on republican principles?—*James Madison, 1787* [43]

> We have as the main voting groups in Southern politics 1) country clubbers, 2) populists [those who feel that too much power rests in too few hands], 3) blacks....
> The class struggle in the South continues, with the populists serving as the trump card. ... In 1982, we discovered we could not hold the populist vote on economic issues alone. When social and cultural issues died down, the populists were left with no compelling reason to vote Republican.... When Republicans are successful in getting certain social issues [i.e. anti-abortion, crime, etc.] to the forefront, the populist vote is ours.—*Lee Atwater, Reagan campaign strategist, 1984* [44]

US AGAINST THEM

One direct result of the denial of social inequality is the outbreak of personal crises brought on by self-blame. Social psychologists have documented self-blame in increased rates of alcoholism, drug abuse, suicides, and domestic violence, and in stress-related illnesses such as heart disease and cancer.[45] Many people find convenient targets for pent-up rage and frustration in scapegoats, such as racial minorities, immigrants, and "welfare cheats." Recruits to neofascist organizations are mostly young white men who are either unemployed or underemployed. The majority of victims of street crime and drug violence are, like the perpetrators, poor people.

Meanwhile, with the rise of anti-union sentiment that accompanies the fear of economic insecurity, the public's organized lines of defense are collapsing. The trade union movement is eroding quickly—down from 32.5 percent of the labor force in 1953 to 15.8 percent in 1992 (11.5 percent in the private sector), another consequence of the decline of solidarity among employed and unemployed workers. Employers are freed to step up benefit cuts: strong and enforceable health and safety protections for workers, adequate minimum wage, parental leave policies, adequate employment compensation, and other basic services are deemed excessive. Workers find little or no support among lawmakers.

Democracy is another casualty. The United States has the lowest voter turnout of any major industrialized country. While the Republicans and Democrats argue over who really represents the middle class, the same moneyed interests give to both parties, hedging their bets. Candidates or parties who express explicitly pro-working class themes are branded as "fringe elements" or "special interests" and excluded from media and party platforms through which they might make their case to the people. In 1984, Jesse Jackson was belittled by the mainstream press and politicians as being too liberal for most Americans. His campaign was effectively blocked, even though most of his campaign themes were closer than his opponents' to public sentiments expressed in numerous opinion polls.[46]

In electoral politics and in interest group campaigning, money talks—so loudly it is nearly impossible to be heard over the noise it makes. Corporations are spending hundreds of millions on advertising, lobbying, and fake "grassroots" campaigns organized to support their interests. The result is an electorate that is heavily skewed to the high end of the economic heap, with the natural effect that elected officials show more and more open disdain, and even hostility, toward the poor and "lower middle." Small wonder, then, that in the last several presidential elections non-voters have made up the largest part of the electorate.

A great deal of time and energy has gone into "fixing" poverty, not by solving problems that bring it about, but by explaining it away. The next chapter will take us down the twisted road built by our poverty experts, leading to that foregone conclusion.

2

DECIDING WHO'S POOR

Growing up in the 1950s, we who thought of ourselves as "middle class" were often bribed by our parents into eating vegetables with the warning that "children are starving in China." Though we couldn't figure out how our eating broccoli would help starving Chinese children, we got the message: poverty and hunger were frightening conditions that only happened to people in other, "underdeveloped" countries.

A rude awakening came in 1962, with the publication of Michael Harrington's *The Other America*.[1] Harrington, a social scientist, had uncovered vast numbers of people in the United States who were suffering from malnutrition, even starvation, as severe as anything in the third world. It was Harrington's assessment that fully 35 million people (about one-fifth of the U.S. population at the time) lived in poverty. *The Other America*, which was read by President John Kennedy, exposed the underside of the post-World War II boom economy so carefully hidden in the 1950s.

Suddenly, poverty and malnutrition were no longer "over there," but visible in our very midst. Neither blind fate nor underdevelopment could explain 35 million people living desperately in such a rich country.[2] Within two years of the publication of *The Other America*, a national "poverty index"—a standard by which to measure who was and was not "poor"—had been devised by the federal government, and President Lyndon Johnson had declared an "unconditional war on poverty."

The new national attention brought into focus a variety of forms of poverty. Some lived in absolute physical deprivation. This level of poverty could be found among African-Americans living in the Mississippi Delta and white Americans of Scotch-Irish descent living in Appalachia—parts of West Virginia, Kentucky, Tennessee, Pennsylvania. Others—immigrant farmworkers from Mexico and the Caribbean, who cut the nation's sugarcane and picked the vegetables and fruit—lived lives of indentured servitude. Still others, living in cities like New York and Chicago, sometimes had television sets and enough food to keep from being malnourished, but had income levels low enough to qualify for certain kinds of government poor relief.

If the poor lived in such dramatically contrasting conditions, what, then, was poverty? In the 1950s we thought we knew *what* it was and *where*. In the 1960s it wasn't so easy to tell. We were discovering that "poverty" and "the poor" are slippery concepts whose meanings have changed over time and in different cultural contexts. For example, the Native Americans encountered by the European colonizers in the seventeenth century had no words for poverty or underdevelopment in their vocabulary. According to Black Hawk, Chief of the Sauk and Fox:

> We always had plenty; our children never cried from hunger, neither were our people in want.... The rapids of Rock River furnished us with an abundance of excellent fish, and the land being very fertile, never failed to produce good crops of corn, beans, pumpkins, and squashes.... Our village was healthy and

there was no place in the country possessing such advantages, nor hunting grounds better than those we had in possession.[3]

Yet, because Native Americans had none of the material goods possessed by the Europeans, the colonizers thought them "primitive," "savage," and "uncivilized"—the seventeenth century equivalents of "underdeveloped." By twentieth—century standards, however, the Europeans who settled this continent—even the wealthiest—would surely be counted among the poor.

In much of the industrialized world today, "poverty" evokes a series of negative images. Nobody wants to be caught in poverty, nor will many admit to being poor. Poverty is often associated with laziness, immorality, ignorance, and criminality. But among certain religious subcultures, poverty is perceived as a virtue and even welcomed. Iranian Sufis, Indian Gandhians, Buddhist monks, and some Roman Catholic priests and nuns regard being poor as an opportunity to live the righteous life. The prophet of Islam, Mohammed, has been quoted as saying, "poverty is my pride and glory,"[4] while Jesus proclaimed the poor "blessed" and declared that they would inherit the earth.

Most people would agree that a person who is deprived of the necessities of subsistence—food to maintain basic nourishment, minimal clothing for warmth, and shelter from the elements—is poor. This definition is reflected in a recent United Nations description of poverty: "Towards the end of the 1980s, in thirty-eight out of 103 developing countries the average person was deficient in daily per capita dietary energy supply."[5]

This is poverty as *absolute deprivation of the resources needed to sustain life* and is the way most people thought of poverty prior to the twentieth century (even though science had not yet learned to define the specific necessary caloric intake).[6] Today, this is still the way poverty is understood in countries with very low per capita incomes.

However, in much of the contemporary world poverty is thought of in relative terms—as deprivation in relation to some culturally defined *standard of need*. That need is not limited to basic material resources but may include social factors of life such as status and self-esteem, as well as access to education, jobs, credit, political power, or a certain level of income.

Scholars who look at poverty in relative terms use a wide range of definitions, depending on what particular societies consider normal and how they measure resources. For example, a person with an annual income under $7,363 in the United States in 1993 was considered poor by the U.S. government. But in a country like El Salvador, where the average manufacturing worker makes $915 a year, a person earning over $7,000 would be considered quite well off.[7]

The very fact that we talk in terms of standards and deficits from standards, however, implies inequality. In turn, inequality implies different measures of political and economic power. In many traditional communal societies (like those of the Native Americans encountered by the early colonists) there was no concept of poverty because such societies shared and distributed their resources among the entire tribe or band. On the other hand, Europeans, coming from stratified class societies, also had a highly developed concept of inequality. Take, for example, the values given to the terms "civilized" and "savage." One historical study notes:

> Conceptions of "savagery" which developed in the sixteenth and seventeenth centuries ... became the common property of Western European culture ... [These conceptions] constituted a distorting lens through which the early colonists assessed the potential and predicted the fate of the non-European peoples they encountered.... What most commonly differentiated civilized or semi-civilized human beings from savages was that they practiced sedentary agriculture, had political forms that Europeans recognized as regular governments, and lived to some extent in urban concentrations.[8]

THE POLITICS OF PERCEPTION

As we have seen, poverty, even in highly unequal societies, is recognized as a social problem that requires a social solution only in specific situations—depending on the underlying value system and the contending political forces in the society. The same goes for how poverty is officially defined and measured once it has been recognized. Recognition, definition, and measurement, then, are political acts that can say a lot about the underlying political power dynamics of a society: who has it, who wants it, and who it is used against. Public acknowledgment of the problem, definition, and measurement also affect whether or not the poor will get government help, and if so, how much and in what form.

Before President Johnson initiated his War on Poverty in 1964, the U.S. government had no means of measuring poverty. In fact, poverty had not been acknowledged as a public problem since the Great Depression, and then, it took the near collapse of the economic system for those in power to admit that large numbers of people were poor. After World War II, and until the early 1960s, the nation's leaders again preferred to ignore the inequality that continued to exist.

With the 1950s came the postwar economic upsurge. Under intense government pressure, the labor movement purged its own left wing and settled into a routine contractual arrangement with management in which collective bargaining for higher wages and better work conditions and benefits became a given. A new sense of security set in for a large (and mostly white) sector of the working class. Roosevelt-era safety nets like the G.I. bill for returning veterans, Social Security for retiring workers, and unemployment insurance to cushion workers in recessions bolstered the workers' sense of inclusion in the social contract. Life was still tough, but the promise of better days was coming true for millions.

Yet poverty was still present and widespread. Racial and economic segregation isolated the destitute in urban ghettos and rural enclaves as effectively as if they were locked away in prison. Without public advocates to call attention to their plight and without political power in the state and federal legislatures, the poor remained voiceless and invisible. The first major challenge came in the form of the civil rights movement that

spread across the South starting in the mid-1950s. The Democratic Party owed black voters for John Kennedy's narrow election victory in 1960. The growing pressure compelled the
Kennedy and Johnson administrations to recognize that poverty
was a national problem. They set out to determine what standards were "adequate" and who fell below them. On this definition would hinge the flow of millions of dollars in federal
programs and subsidies.

HOW POOR IS POOR?

Mollie Orshansky, an economist with the Social Security Administration under President Johnson, is credited with developing the formula for determining what was an adequate standard
of need. Ironically, while Orshansky developed this standard
only as a research tool, the government adopted it as its major
means of identifying who is eligible for government poor support.[9] It is expressed as the annual income required to achieve a
minimal, but sufficient, standard of living. The base income level
rises with the number of people in a family, is adjusted for
persons over sixty-five, and is indexed on a yearly basis to rises
in the Consumer Price Index (used as a measure of inflation). In
1993, the poverty index for a family of four was $14,763, and for
a person living alone, $7,518.[10] (We will return to Orshansky's
formula later in this chapter.)

The government considers anyone with an income below its
poverty line to be poor, while anyone above it is nonpoor. For
purposes of providing welfare grants and other government
subsidies, the states have defined their own standards of need,
which vary from the federal standard. The federal poverty index
provides the base line for determining both the state of the
nation's inequality and most of the government help that is
provided to the poor.

Each year in March, the Census Bureau takes a survey of
60,000 households to determine how many people fall above and
below the poverty line. It does this by asking a sample of people

to disclose their previous year's pretax incomes. This income includes wages and salaries, net income from self-employment, dividends, interest, royalty and net rental income, Social Security and welfare payments, pensions, and income from other sources such as alimony. It excludes, however, profits made from buying and selling stocks and bonds (called capital gains), as well as the value of such noncash benefits as employer-provided health insurance, food stamps, or Medicaid (the last two being government food and medical subsidies for people with low incomes). Later, a series of *Current Population Reports* gives the number of people living in poverty in the previous year—the year from which the data was collected.[11]

In 1993, the most recent year for which we have such data, there were 39.3 million people living below the official government poverty level, or 15.1 percent of the population. The actual number of people living in poverty was the highest since 1962, when 38.6 million were officially designated as poor, although the *rate* of poverty (that is, the percentage of poor people in the general population) was considerably lower (15 percent in 1993 as compared to 21 percent in 1962).[12]

The percentage of poor people living below the poverty level does not tell the whole story, however. We need to know how much below the level their incomes fell. In 1993, 16 million people—40.7 percent of the poor—lived in families or households whose incomes were below one-half of their respective poverty levels. A slightly smaller number (12.5 million) had "near poor" incomes below 125 percent of the poverty level.[13] Since many poverty researchers (as we will see later on) consider poverty level incomes inadequate to meet basic human needs, these figures indicate that the image of the United States as one big happy middle class is not only a myth but a calculated lie.

In fact, *the majority of poor people are white, and live in intact families whose head participates in the labor market.* However, if you are African-American, Latino, female, under eighteen, or living in a female-headed family, your chances of living in poverty increase dramatically.

Racial, Gender, and Age Characteristics of People Living in Poverty, 1993 (by percent)

Poverty Rate by Race

All Persons	*15.1*
White	12.2
Asian and Pacific Islander	15.3
Hispanic origin	30.6
African-American	33.1

Poverty Rate by Gender and Race

All Males	*13.3*
White	10.7
Hispanic origin	27.6
African-American	29.7
All Females	*16.9*
White	13.7
Hispanic origin	33.6
African-American	29.7

Poverty Rate by Age and Race

All Persons Over 65	*12.2*
White	10.7
Hispanic origin	21.4
African-American	28.0
All Persons Under 18	*17.8*
White	17.8
Hispanic origin	40.9
African-American	46.1

Not only are higher proportions of African-Americans and Latinos poor, but in comparison to whites in poverty, they are *much poorer*. The sector of the white poor with incomes of 50 percent or less of the poverty level came in at 4.5 percent, while 10.5 percent of the Latino poor and 16.7 percent of poor African-Americans were at rock bottom.[14]

More women than men are poor, and there are almost twice as many poor children as there are poor elderly. When race is added to youth, the poverty burden on children shoots up. Almost 50 percent of African-American children under the age of eighteen lived in poverty in 1993 and more than 40 percent of all Latino children did. This gives the United States the highest child poverty rate of any modern industrialized nation![15]

Families with children were more likely to be poor regardless of the work experience of adults in the household. It should be noted that without Social Security benefits, which push many of the elderly just over the poverty line, many more would be officially poor. Nearly 20 percent of the elderly lived below 125 percent of the poverty line in 1993 and more than one out of four lived below 150 percent. Single female-headed families suffered more poverty than other types; 38.7 percent of such families were poor in 1993, compared with 13.6 percent of all families and 8.0 percent of married-couple families. When only single female-headed families with children under eighteen are counted, the poverty rate rises to 53.7 percent.[16]

THE DISAPPEARING CHILDHOOD OF THE POOR

A fourth-grade classroom on a forbidding stretch of the South Side was in the middle of multiplication tables when a voice over the intercom ordered Nicholas Whitiker to the principal's office.... It was yet another time that the adult world called on Nicholas, a gentle, brooding

10-year-old, to be a man, to answer for the complicated universe he calls family....

How could he begin to explain his reality—that his mother, a welfare recipient rearing five young children, was in college trying to become a nurse and so was not home during the day, that [Nicholas's sister] Ishtar's father was separated from his mother and in a drug-and-alcohol haze most of the time, that the grandmother he used to live with was at work, and that, besides, he could not possibly account for the man who was supposed to take his sister home—his mother's companion, the father of her youngest child?....

Of all the men in his family's life, Nicholas is perhaps the most dutiful. When the television picture goes out again, when the 3-year-old scratches the 4-year-old, when their mother, Angela, needs ground beef from the store or the bathroom cleaned or can't find her switch to whip him or the other children, it is Nicholas's name that rings out to fix whatever is wrong.... He is nanny, referee, housekeeper, handyman. Some nights up past midnight, mopping the floors, putting the children to bed and washing their school clothes in the bathtub. It is a nightly chore: the children have few clothes and wear the same thing every day.—*New York Times*[17]

Poverty appears unevenly from region to region as well, with the South the poorest area overall. Within large cities there are areas whose conditions rival those of the third world. Inner-city neighborhoods with heavy concentrations of African-Americans, Latinos, and new immigrants, especially from Latin America and Asia, have higher levels of poverty in comparison with the entire metropolitan area.[18] Mortality rates in New York City's central Harlem are higher than those in Bangladesh.

ROCK BOTTOM

Jonestown, Miss. This forlorn little town of rickety shotgun shacks and 1,467 people, surrounded by the table-top-flat cotton fields of northeast Mississippi, has the spent air of a place that history has passed by.... Small towns that were once economically stable and racially mixed are becoming pockets of poverty and overwhelmingly black—75 to 100 percent so.... The pattern is so striking that some experts say a new kind of ghetto is evolving: rural instead of urban, but sharing many conditions of the inner city: white flight, black poverty, a disappearing job base, reliance on government welfare payments, rising crime and social isolation.—*New York Times*[19]

Although urban poverty is more concentrated (and therefore more visible), the rural Mississippi Delta, Appalachia, many Native American reservations, and the backwoods of Maine have always had some of the most abject poverty in the nation.[20] Over the last twenty years, family farms have given way to more profitable agribusiness enterprises, contributing to an ever-shrinking job market. The rural poor have little or no pull with elected representatives; of all national sectors, they are least likely to benefit from federal poverty programs. Deep Southern states like Mississippi provide some of the lowest welfare payments in the country.

HOMELESS IN THE HEARTLAND

[The] Housing Assistance Council, a rural advocacy group in Washington, found that rural people accounted for a fourth of all stays in homeless shelters in 2,200 rural and urban counties it surveyed across the country last year. The problem is even more acute in heavily agricultural states like South Dakota, where rural people account for close to 90 percent of the state's 4,000 homeless.... "They try to keep it secret as long as they can," said Margaretann Sweet, a psychologist who counsels homeless people in Charlotte, Michigan. "Some are ashamed to tell their friends they've lost their farm. Owning land and working hard to keep it is central to self-esteem here." "Some of them have attempted suicide before coming into the city because, for them, coming to the city means failure," said Sue Watlow Phillips, who heads the Minnesota Coalition for the Homeless.—*New York Times* [21]

The poverty statistics also indicate that, rather than living off the earnings of others—as so much anti-welfare talk has it—poor people work for pay. One study found that 40.9 percent of the officially poor sixteen years and older worked during 1993, and 9.7 percent worked year-round, full-time.[22] In 1992, 18 percent of those working full-time earned less than the poverty level for a family of four. This is a rise of 50 percent in the last thirteen years! Although these wage trends affect all segments of the population, they are particularly sharp for younger workers and those without college educations.[23]

These figures, of course, include only those whose incomes fell below the official poverty line. Critics of the poverty index point out that millions of people who work full-time still can't afford the basic necessities—food, clothing, shelter, medical care—even at the lowest realistic cost.[24] Yet because of the inadequacy of the poverty standard, they are not counted as poor. Expenses such as extraordinary health care bills or even tax payments may bring the disposable after-tax incomes of such people below the poverty level.

WORKING, BUT STILL POOR

Bruce and Sarah Lanier are both high school graduates. Residents of Grand Rapids, Michigan, Bruce works full time as a carpenter and Sarah half time as a retail-store sales clerk. They are raising twin daughters, now 11 years old, on a combined income of $19,700, which puts them nearly 50 percent above the Census Bureau's poverty line. Yet, they cannot afford a telephone, and most months there are times when they either skip meals or must "borrow" from relatives or friends to pay for food. They walk several miles each way to work when they have too little money to fix their fourteen-year-old car. They have no medical insurance, and the twins have never been to a dentist. When they cannot pay their utility bills, their heat is turned off, sometimes in the cold of winter.... There are millions of families like the Laniers that the Census Bureau [when it counts the "poor"] completely ignores.—*The Nation* [25]

DEFINITION AND MEASUREMENT

From its very beginnings in the 1960s, the poverty index has been the subject of political controversy. At issue is the extent to which fiscal (taxing and spending) policies should be used to redistribute income from the wealthy to those more or less in need. The public's perception of poverty is crucial to the outcome of this battle. If the percentage of those classified as poor is large, the public will tend to perceive poverty as a major social problem requiring government action. This could take the form of increased welfare payments, low-income housing subsidies, and other programs, all of which may require higher taxes. If the numbers are small, the public will have other priorities, such as reducing taxes.

As a result, Republicans and conservatives, ideologically opposed to the government transferring wealth downward, have tried to minimize the number of poor, while Democrats and liberals have argued for a somewhat larger percentage.

Advocates for the poor want to see the numbers set even higher, the better to push for more radical reforms in the distribution of economic resources, such as full employment and generous welfare programs.

Just how was the poverty index first determined? The figure of $14,763 for a family of four is a somewhat arbitrary amount—but not one simply pulled out of a hat. In order to be considered viable, the poverty index had to be based on some politically acceptable criteria of costs.

Mollie Orshansky walked a fine line in setting the index.[26] She knew that congressional conservatives were waiting to pounce and that the numbers would have to reflect a compromise with them. But having grown up in a poor family, she knew that the figures she would agree to could mean that many of those who needed government help would be left without it—especially single urban mothers and their children.[27]

The President's Council of Economic Advisors had originally proposed a flat $3,000 poverty line, no matter what the size or condition of the family.[28] Orshansky saw that such an arbitrary figure would benefit farm families and older families, since farm families grew much of their own food and older people did not need as much. However, it seriously underestimated the needs of younger and larger urban families. She therefore tried to come up with a formula that was related to the "average" standard of living in the United States and that could be adjusted for family size and type.

Orshansky knew that the Department of Agriculture (USDA) had taken a survey of food consumption in 1955 which showed that, on average, families of three or more spent about one-third of their income on food. By multiplying the cost of an average basket of food by three, she would come up with an adequate standard of need. Orshansky also knew that the USDA had previously developed four different average food budgets, ranging from the minimal nutrient intake needed to sustain a family for about two months (known as the Economy Food Plan) to much more generous market baskets. She therefore proposed two different poverty indexes, one based on the Economy Food Plan and the other on the USDA's slightly more generous (and nutritionally better) "Low-Cost Food Plan." Each of these plans was multiplied by three and the resulting poverty index was then adjusted for family size and type (i.e., number in family and age of family head). Deliberations over the measurement of poverty followed. The Office of Economic Opportunity (the special unit set up to coordinate the War on Poverty) adopted the poverty index that was based on the least expensive food plan. The result, of course, was that the number of people living "in poverty" was assessed as less than it would have been if the index had been based on the more nutritionally adequate food plan. The original poverty line was equal to about one-half the median family income in 1964, the same relative standard that most other industrialized countries use as their measure of poverty.

How accurate is the current poverty index in measuring the real extent of economic suffering and inequality in the nation? The most obvious problem with a standard based on a *national average* of household spending is that the cost of living differs from region to region and from city to city. In Newark, New Jersey, a fair market rent (FMR) for a two-bedroom apartment was $765 a month in 1993; in rural South Carolina the FMR for a similar apartment was $341.[29] A single baseline may thus *underestimate* the extent of poverty in expensive cities and *overestimate* it in less expensive regions.

In 1994, the General Accounting Office (the independent agency that controls and monitors congressional spending) recommended that poverty rates be adjusted by state to reflect both differences in the cost of living and each state's ability to raise revenues. But Southern members of Congress know that this formula would lose them federal money to states with higher costs of living.[30]

The poverty index may have misrepresented the proportion of the budget that the poor actually spent on food. Since the poor have less disposable income (money available for use) than anyone else, they tend to spend a higher proportion of their income on fixed expenses like housing and transportation. Recent evidence suggests that over a third of the poor spend a huge 70 percent of their incomes on housing alone.[31] This means that poor people today often have to choose between feeding their families and paying rent—a major cause of homelessness.

The poverty line is adjusted up or down to the Consumer Price Index (CPI). The CPI is based on a national survey of the costs of a variety of goods and services purchased by the average urban household. Some argue this inflates the number of classifiably poor people. The best-known example: prior to 1983, there had been an excessive growth in the CPI due to an inflationary housing market in the late 1970s. The Census Bureau corrected this by adjusting the way it measures changes in housing costs. However, since the effect of adjusting poverty thresholds for inflation is cumulative, a lower measure of *past* inflation carries over, resulting in a lower poverty threshold in the *present*. The Census Bureau has determined that if this past distortion were taken into account, the current thresholds would be approximately 8 percent lower and fewer people would be classified as poor.[32]

This is valid in theory. But Bureau of Labor Statistics data suggest that from 1967 to 1982, the overall cost of basic necessities, like food, shelter, utilities, and medical care may have risen faster than the revised CPI. Using the CPI, then, will not adjust the poverty line enough to compensate for the actual price increases faced by the poor. So even after adjusting downward for inflation, the poverty line must be revised upward still further.[33]

After two revisions, the basic formula remains the same: the cost of the least expensive USDA food plan multiplied by three. As we have seen, this formula was based on surveys of spending taken in the 1950s.[34] From the start, the food budget used as a base for the multiplier was an inadequate reflection of a family's long-term nutrient needs. Today, the average family pays proportionately more of its budget for such items as housing, child care, and transportation than it did in the 1950s.

By 1993, the original four-person family poverty budget was only 39.9 percent of the median family income for a four-person family, an approximately 10 percentage point drop in the poverty standard! In effect, the poverty line has been transformed from one pegged to average living standards into an absolute standard, contradicting Orshansky's original intention when she devised it.[35] Liberal critics have suggested that the food budget should be increased to one that is nutritionally adequate over the long term, and that the multiplier should be increased to more than three to reflect changes in the relative proportions of household budget items. These changes would result in a considerably higher poverty line.

Most Americans, when polled, say they would draw the poverty line higher than the government does.[36] The public's perception about how much it costs to survive is borne out by a study conducted by economist Patricia Ruggles for the Joint Economic Committee of Congress. She concluded that the current U.S. poverty level would have to be at least 50 percent higher than it is at present to reflect changes in consumption standards.[37] Ironically, the government's eligibility requirements for certain noncash programs, such as food stamps, Medicaid, free school lunches, and housing subsidies, have reflected its own recognition of the inadequacy of the poverty line. Most of these programs (before the cuts of 1995) were available to people whose incomes fell below or only came up to a certain percentage above the poverty line.

In addition to the inadequacy of both the food budget and of the multiplier used to determine the poverty line, poverty is undercounted by the Census Bureau. Undercounting occurs when the Census Bureau misses housing units and persons within sample households, as well when it fails to count the homeless or institutionalized. For some groups, such as black males between twenty and twenty-four years old, the undercoverage can be as high as 29 percent.[38] While the bureau attempts to adjust for such undercounting, the final impact on estimates is unknown.

The problem of undercounting, like the poverty index itself, has been the subject of political debate. Since large amounts of federal government aid to states and cities (as well as political representation in state and federal legislatures) depends on Census Bureau figures, even a change of one percentage point can mean a difference of millions of dollars in federal aid.

Just after the 1990 census, a coalition of big-city mayors and homeless advocates sued in federal court to get the Commerce Department (the parent agency of the Census Bureau) to adjust the 1990 population count to include those who, according to the Census Bureau's own estimates, had been missed. Democratic mayors argued that the largely poor and minority populations in their cities were being deliberately shortchanged by the Republican administration. The suit maintained that the Census Bureau deliberately set out to undercount the homeless "and as a result to reduce the level of funding for programs which would benefit the homeless." The Bush administration, fearing both the financial and political costs of a larger poverty count, argued against the changes sought by the mayors, but the courts were divided.[39] If the Supreme Court decides in favor of the cities, the result will be more funding for the poor, and more congressional seats allocated to cities over suburbs and rural areas.[40]

Finally, respondents' answers to Census Bureau questions are open to distortion. Several studies have found that upper-income groups tend to understate their incomes, especially income from rents, dividends, privately-owned businesses, or professional employment.[41] A recent study by the Census Bureau using the 1992 survey results concluded that their surveys only reported 51 percent of income from interest and only 22 percent from dividends.[42]

Since this kind of income tends to be concentrated among the affluent, such underreporting makes the distribution of income look more evenly spread out than it really is.

LOWERING THE POVERTY LINE

Conservatives claim that the current poverty index *overstates* the case. They have fought (although so far unsuccessfully) to have the dollar value of noncash government transfers (such as food stamps, Medicaid, and government housing subsidies) included in the income used to determine poverty status. If these adjustments are made, conservatives argue, the statistical portrait of the United States would be brighter and we wouldn't have to spend so much for the poor.[43]

Various studies that include the cash value of noncash transfers in calculating the poverty line suggest that doing this cuts the poverty rate by as much as a third. But as usual, figures on paper can be used to justify even more suffering for the poor in real life. In the first place, noncash benefits are not evenly divided among the poor. Medicaid, for example, is used when a person is sick. While a person's standard of living is improved with health care, having a hospital bill paid through a government program is not the same thing as having that money available as disposable income. Furthermore, not all of the benefits of these programs go directly to the poor. Housing contractors, doctors, hospital administrators, case workers, and similar "go-betweens," as conduits for these funds, receive a share—and none of them are poor! Many poor people are not receiving in-kind transfers received by others—but even if they are eligible for the benefits, they are in no way less poor for it.[44]

Meanwhile, if this standard were to be applied across the board, the cash value of all the hidden government subsidies that go to the more affluent would also have to be counted. These include home mortgage deductions, deductions for the maintenance of rental property, depreciation allowances, and the lucrative government contracts and tax abatements that come with being able to win friends and influence people in the political establishment.

THE POLITICS OF COUNTING THE POOR

In 1970 an interagency committee appointed by President Nixon examined the possibility of adding nonmoney income to the base on which the poverty count was taken. This was after the 1970 census had revealed a rise in the number of poor, coming after ten consecutive years of decline. The study was met with public ridicule, as critics of the Administration charged an effort to "end poverty with a stroke of the pen."

Similar efforts were undertaken in 1971 and again in 1973. The third time, the committee even considered doing away with the federal use of the word "poverty." According to a government source interviewed by the *New York Times*, "Poverty is a value-laden, highly politicized word and that's not the kind of word we like. We would like a less value-laden concept like income distribution or mean or median or some other word devoid of emotional complications."—*New York Times*[45]

In a 1990 paper the conservative Heritage Foundation think tank charged the Census Bureau with conducting a Soviet-style "disinformation campaign" to make Americans believe "the living standards of America's 'poor' are far lower than in reality they are."[46] The Reagan and Bush administrations used this argument in their cut-back campaigns.

The Center on Budget and Policy Priorities, a liberal think tank, criticized the Heritage Foundation's attack on the census data as "highly ideological, sometimes careless, and frequently misleading." Heritage, they pointed out, included in income going to the poor billions of dollars in administrative costs, as well as money going to the nonpoor, such as the costs of economic development programs for paving streets or enhancing commercial properties.[47]

Pressured from both left and right, in 1988 the Census Bureau began publishing a separate study of income distribution that includes the effects of taxes, noncash transfers, and net estimated home equity on income levels. In 1993, the bureau's report on income and poverty included fifteen experimental ways of measuring poverty, under which the poverty rate ranged from 11.2 percent to 23.8 percent.[48]

The most fully adjusted income definition—one that included the effect of taxes, cash and noncash benefits, capital gains, employee health benefits, and net return on home equity suggested that a more equal distribution of income exists than is calculated when counting only money income. Despite this, estimates of the number of poor persons increased between 1991 and 1993. In one interesting finding, when the current income measure was modified to exclude government cash transfers (such as those offered to single mothers through Aid to Families with Dependent Children, AFDC), the poverty rate shot up from 15.1 percent to 23.4 percent. By this measure, without such government programs we would have near-Depression levels of destitution in the country.

In April 1995, the National Academy of Sciences recommended major changes in the way the government measures poverty. They said that the government should move toward a concept of poverty based on disposable income and be adjusted for geographic differences in housing costs. Under this proposal, both cash and noncash income would be counted, but taxes, work expenses, child care costs, and out-of-pocket medical expenses would be deducted from cash income. The proposal would raise poverty rates for families with one or more workers and families that lack health care, and lower them somewhat for families that receive various kinds of government assistance. However, the proposal would probably raise the overall poverty rate and thus faces opposition by conservatives.[49]

COUNTING THE UNEMPLOYED

After the poverty index, the most important government indicator of the state of the nation's equality is the unemployment rate. This purports to show what percentage of the nation's working population over the age of sixteen is out of work in a given time period. Since labor is the dominant source of household income, as well as the dominant cost to businesses and governments in producing the nation's goods and services, the unemployment rate is a key indicator of the health of the economy.[50]

Like the poverty rate, the unemployment rate reflects a set of compromises that have resulted from conflicting political pressures on government researchers. First, it is connected to the disbursement of millions of dollars in unemployment compensation for jobless workers. As the rate goes up, the public may pressure government into either increasing unemployment compensation or intervening in the economy in more drastic ways. Intervention could mean investing in job training and placement programs, or actually creating jobs.

Second, the employment rate has been one of the signals to government economists of possible growth in inflation, the other important indicator of the economy's health. Since the 1960s, public policy experts have debated whether low employment is itself inflationary by nature. Many economIsts believe that when employment reaches a certain "natural" level—they call it the "Phillips Curve"—it triggers inflation.[51] They conclude that in managing the nation's economy, a trade-off must be made between inflation and unemployment. This view was opposed by more than one major economist; William Vickrey, former president of the American Economics Association, called the concept of a "natural" rate of unemployment "one of the most vicious euphemisms ever coined."[52]

This did not stop economists at the Federal Reserve System (the public/private agency that influences the nation's credit system and money supply) from acting as if the Phillips Curve was an ironclad law. Since the late 1970s, the Fed's tight money policies (raising the interest rates they charge to banks and instituting other credit-tightening measures) seemed to limit inflation, but they have also been used to justify a twenty-year decline in real wages and a steady increase in the rate of unemployment.[53]

In the spring of 1994, anticipating inflation as the economy began to pull out of a recession, the Federal Reserve raised interest rates seven times in a little over a year, even though inflation was at a twenty-year low. With each new rate increase (resulting in the layoff of thousands), the papers reported that stocks and bonds soared. Wall Street was delighted.[54]

THE UNEMPLOYED: THE NEW "INFLATION FIGHTERS"

When the Fed raises the interest rates it charges to banks, the banks in turn raise the interest rate they charge to customers. This makes it harder for families to buy mortgages, for consumers to pay credit card bills, and for businesses to invest in new plants and equipment and thus to create more jobs. With fewer people buying, firms are compelled to lay off workers; the workers, in turn, cut their spending, reducing employment even further. With millions looking for work, companies can lower wages and cut benefits for those still employed. Thus, the effect of the Fed's tight money policies is a brake on the economy—like opening wounds in the body of the economy to drain out the "bad blood" of excess labor.—*Dollars and Sense*[55]

By now it should be obvious that "prosperity" and "a strong economy" mean two distinct things to government economists. Bankers (who loan money for long periods) and bondholders lose during inflationary periods. Nearly all the officers of the Federal Reserve come from the financial sector and go back into it when they have finished their terms. For them, inflation is a real live threat, while unemployment is a statistical effect. Despite all the ruined lives this arrangement results in, when the public interest is totally opposite that of the financial sector, there's no question of who will win the battle for support in Washington.

THE JOB KILLER

Favor a weak economy? Who would do that? Enter that mysterious and slightly sinister entity, The Bond Market, the preeminent force in the economy today. More than any other group, the bond market's members determine how many Americans will have jobs, whether the jobholders will earn enough to afford a house or a car, or whether a factory might have to lay off workers.... In sum, the American economy is governed by the bond market.... The bond market is a huge storehouse of accumulated wealth—a giant vault, so to speak, from which saved money is loaned out not for a few weeks or months, but for years at a time.

Those multi-year loans totaled more than $10 trillion at the end of last year, according to the Federal Reserve's most recent data. That is a huge sum. If the $10 trillion were somehow to disappear, refilling the vault would absorb the entire national income—all wages, salaries and profits—for a year and a half.

Naturally, when they lend from the vault, the people who own the $10 trillion, or their agents ... want it paid back intact, undiminished by inflation. And keeping down inflation has come to mean weakening the economy.—*New York Times*[56]

According to the Bureau of Labor Statistics, 6 percent of the population, or almost eight million people, were counted as officially unemployed in May 1994. Economist Allen H. Meltzer of the Carnegie-Mellon Institute, who endorsed the Fed's decision to raise interest rates, didn't think eight million unemployed people were stuck without jobs: "They are really all people between jobs."[57]

Is it possible that all eight million unemployed were really *between* jobs? More specifically, how well does the unemployment rate measure the nation's joblessness? As in our analysis of the poverty index, we have to look at how the government collects data and defines unemployment.

Each month the Census Bureau conducts a survey of a sample of 60,000 households for the Bureau of Labor Statistics (BLS), asking a series of questions desired to get at the work status and experience of respondents.[58] The BLS then translates this data into a measure of unemployment.[59]

"The unemployed" usually means everyone who is out of full-time work; some narrow it down to those jobless who are looking for a full-time job. But this is *not* how the government defines it. First, the Labor Department counts as "employed" everyone working one or more hours a week, for pay or profit (or fifteen hours of unpaid work in a family business). Even if people are working part-time, but want (and need) full-time work, they are counted as "employed." To be counted as "unem-ployed," a person must have been fired or laid off from a waged or salaried job—to have lost employment as a result of a self-owned business doesn't count—and be *actively* looking for work in the four weeks prior to the week the survey was conducted. (This means contacting employers and employment agencies, not just reading want ads or getting work training.)

Left out of the "unemployed" category, therefore, are millions of people who can't make a go of self-employment. These include people who have lost jobs but have become so discouraged that they've given up looking for work, people who want to start working but have not been able to find a job and have given up (a disproportionate number of minority youth and displaced homemakers), and people with disabling conditions or sick rel-atives, who would take a job if supportive services were avail-able. Also left out are more than one million men and women in the prison system—the majority of whom are from groups with high unemployment rates, such as young African-American and Latino men.

None of these people are counted as either employed or unemployed; they simply don't exist in the employment picture. As Michael Yates has pointed out, because of these definitions the unemployment rate actually *falls* when unemployed people stop looking for work![60] This has prompted the National Urban League, the Council on International and Public Affairs, and other organizations to call for a revised and expanded definition of joblessness.

THE *REAL* JOBLESS RATE

At the end of 1994, the BLS reported that 7.2 million people were officially jobless. An expanded concept of unemployment would have included not only the officially jobless, but 4.4 million persons who wanted full-time jobs but were involuntarily forced to settle for part-time work, and 5.6 million who wanted jobs but were not actively looking for them either because they were discouraged or had disabilities or home responsibilities. Altogether over 17 million people should have been counted as unemployed.[61]

There's more. Some conservatives have argued that the official unemployment rate is too high. They have called for the government to count everyone employed in the underground economy—those earning income derived from both legal and illegal activities that are not reported to the IRS. While millions of people who are not counted as either employed or unemployed make some kind of living in the underground economy, the extent of this activity and its affects on the unemployment rate are very hard to measure. Private and government estimates of the size of this economy have ranged from 5 to 33 percent of GNP.[62] However, what draws people to the dangerous side—for example, selling illegal guns and drugs, as well as "under-the-counter" payment—is precisely the lack of jobs at decent wages. The very existence of the underground economy, then, would be called into question if the above-ground economy were to provide economic security for everyone.

What do examinations of both the poverty index and unemployment rates tell us about our country? First, the exclusion from official definitions of as many as half of those who suffer economically show how statistics, along with the myth of class-lessness, are used to mask the grim realities of poverty and inequality in the United States. Second, this picture reveals how, for the powers that be, the primary value is not the life quality of the majority but the wealth of its most prominent sectors. Third, from the beginning of our society, only massive political activity by those most adversely affected by the government's economic policies have brought changes in the public perception of the problem and generated any public policies aimed at solutions.

3

FROM THEORY TO POLICY

Historically, societies structured on inequality have tended to view poverty as part of the natural order. In India, for example, Hindus believe that the poor are born into a lower caste as a condition of the working out of bad karma from previous lives. In medieval Europe, the serfs, who lived at the bottom of the social and economic pyramid, were thought to be ordained by God to occupy their place in the divinely ordered "Great Chain of Being."

With the emergence of capitalism in Europe, however, poverty could no longer be rationalized as God's will. Capitalism and the rise of science over religious doctrine set in place the idea that people can improve the condition into which they are born through hard work, sacrifice, delayed gratification, and in more recent times, education. But the persistence of poverty—and the patterns of some groups staying poor while others found ways to prosper—was not easily explained away.

Slaveholders justified the dehumanization of Africans by giving the old divine order of creation a racial basis. Biblical passages referring to "hewers of wood and haulers of water" were used to justify the enslavement of Africans as ordained by God. But as white craftsmen were drawn into the new industrial work-force based on the wage system, an explanation had to be found for the rise of poverty in the midst of the material abundance made possible by capitalism.

From early in the nineteenth century to well into the second half of the twentieth, social policy was based on a distinction between the "deserving" and "undeserving."[1] This distinction was based on the ever-popular notion that opportunity for productive work is available to all. The "deserving poor" were those people—mainly widows and their children, the elderly, the sick and infirm—who were thought to be poor through no fault of their own. The able-bodied poor, on the other hand, were considered to have some default of character: they were rogues, vagabonds, drunks, lazy, or simply incompetent. The deserving poor were entitled to private charity or public relief; the undeserving poor, on the other hand, got punishment, most often in the form of the poorhouse—a semi-prison in which the poor were made to work off the cost of their care in a variety of menial jobs.[2]

In time, however, the label of "undeserving" spread from the able-bodied to the great majority of poor people. As Michael B. Katz, a historian of poverty policy, put it,

> The redefinition of poverty as a moral condition ... served to justify the mean-spirited treatment of the poor, which in turn checked expenses for poor relief and provided a powerful incentive to work. In this way the moral definition of poverty helped ensure the supply of cheap labor in a market economy increasingly based on unbound wage labor.[3]

According to Katz, the moral stigma attached to poverty survived even the Great Depression, when millions of hardworking people were plunged into poverty. As a result, the unemployed were reluctant to seek state help and turned to it only as a last resort.[4] The New Deal programs erected during that period continued to distinguish between the deserving and undeserving poor.

With the "rediscovery" of poverty in the 1960s, politicians increasingly turned to social scientists for explanations, for advice in shaping policy, and for data to back up their programs.[5] Many social scientists were able to win power and prestige, including government grants and recognition as the "experts" who could be called on by government. This career track could even lead to top level appointments and elective office. Daniel Patrick Moynihan, a Harvard professor of sociology and later a U.S. senator, and Robert Reich, a Harvard political economist and later Clinton's labor secretary, are well-known examples. Others who argued that government services had led to a "dysfunctional social welfare state" rode the crest of a conservative Republican wave to become heavy hitters in policymaking from the late 1970s through the 1990s.

Since the 1960s, conservatives, liberals, Marxists, socialists, feminists, black nationalists, and even New Age cultists have all joined the debate over poverty. Dozens of new research institutes and think tanks have sprung up to support the work of poverty theorists.

In this chapter we will examine the major "schools" of poverty theory and the policy directions that are suggested by them. Each of these schools and the individuals associated with them can be identified by the degree to which they emphasize the role of socioeconomic systems in creating and affecting poverty or the behavior and attitudes of the poor. Those who more strongly emphasize the role of systems are the ones who naturally call for systemic transformation. Those who emphasize behavior call for educating, coercing, or punishing the poor. One theorist, Charles Murray, goes beyond the behavior and attitudes of the poor to place the blame for poverty on genetics.

THE CONTEXT OF POVERTY RESEARCH

In the early 1960s, Michael Harrington's *The Other America* uncovered a variety of types of poverty. Since then, however, poverty theory has come to focus almost exclusively on inner-city

African-Americans and Latinos. Indeed, terms like the "persistently poor" (Oscar Lewis) the "lower class" (Edward Banfield), and the "underclass" (Ken Auletta, Julius Wilson) are used as seemingly innocent code words to refer to these population groups.

Most of the poverty theorists and those who fund their work are white. While most poor people are rural and white, the poor areas closest to the centers of education are disproportionately African-American and Latino urban neighborhoods. Rural poverty is more diffuse, and usually hidden from the academic centers.

Attention to urban poverty is also a direct result of the civil rights movement. With the defeat of Southern Jim Crow laws enforcing legal segregation, Dr. Martin Luther King, Jr. and others turned their attention to the other barriers to full equality across the nation: slum housing; inadequate income for single-parent families; lack of access to good jobs in formerly closed labor markets, and the like.[6] Just before his assassination, King was organizing a massive "Poor People's Campaign" aimed at bringing the poor to the center of power.

The eruption of riots in more than 100 ghettos across the country in 1964 and again in 1967 brought intensified recognition of urban poverty. Some viewed these events as explosions of crime, others as more political "urban rebellions." But no one could deny that, suddenly, social peace had a higher price tag than before.

A presidential commission sought to uncover the causes of the unrest, bringing to the forefront the facts previously ignored or denied; namely the relationship between poverty, inner-city conditions, and racism. That commission's report framed the situation with these famous words:

> Our nation is moving toward two societies, one black, one white—separate and unequal.... To pursue our present course will involve the continuing polarization of the American community and, ultimately, the destruction of basic democratic values.[7]

This increased awareness of racial injustice appeared alongside a new media image of urban crime that permanently linked race, poverty, and violence.

THE CULTURE OF POVERTY

The earliest groups of social scientists to study the poor during the 1960s were anthropologists, sociologists, and political scientists who developed what has come to be known as the "culture of poverty" thesis. These included prominent anthropologist Oscar Lewis, sociologist Daniel Patrick Moynihan, and political scientist Edward Banfield.[8]

Culture of poverty theorists hold that people who are persistently poor are culturally different in their behavior, values, and attitudes from the majority—described as middle-class mainstream—and even from other people who might be just as materially deprived but who still retain middle-class values and attitudes. Based on cross-national ethnographic studies, Oscar Lewis tried to show that about 20 percent of the *objectively* poor had developed a subculture that kept them from changing their condition.

This subculture was defined by as many as seventy interrelated social, economic, and psychological traits, which Lewis claimed were passed down from generation to generation, preventing subsequent generations from taking advantage of openings for upward mobility.[9] These traits included: an attitude of fatalism and low aspirations; low literacy rates; isolation from mainstream institutions and a hostile attitude toward them; common-law marriages; early initiation into sex; living for instant gratifications; little or no organizational life; and a high tendency to drop out of school.

Lewis traced this subculture to a set of socioeconomic-political conditions:

(1) a cash economy, wage labor and production for profit; (2) a persistently high rate of unemployment and underemployment for unskilled labor; (3) low wages; (4) the failure to provide social,

political and economic organization ... for the low-income population; (5) the existence of a bilateral kinship system rather than a unilateral one; and finally, (6) the existence of a set of values in the dominant classes which stresses the accumulation of wealth and property, the possibility of upward mobility and thrift, and explains low economic status as the result of personal inadequacy or inferiority.[10]

The solution he envisioned was the self-organization of the poor to struggle for their rights as a class. "When the poor become class-conscious or active members of trade-union organizations," he wrote, "they are no longer part of the culture of poverty, although they still may be desperately poor."[11]

Lewis contended that his objective in portraying this subculture was to create a more sympathetic view of the poor and their problems among social service workers and policy makers. If the poor were better understood, he felt, more effective antipoverty policy would be produced.[12]

In 1965, Daniel Moynihan, then assistant secretary of labor in the Johnson administration, wrote a confidential study, *The Negro Family: The Case for National Action*.[13] The study grew out of Moynihan's belief that a rise of female-headed families in poor black communities should be a central concern for Johnson's War on Poverty.[14]

Moynihan maintained that female-headed families cause a "tangle of pathology" in the ghetto: high unemployment and school drop-out rates; teen pregnancy; family violence; and criminal behavior. He argued that the fabric of family life there had been so torn that "unless this damage is repaired, all the effort to end discrimination and poverty and injustice will come to little."[15]

Where Lewis relied on ethnographic studies of single families or communities, Moynihan sought to bolster his thesis with statistical data: two decades' worth of statistics on out-of-wedlock births, AFDC caseloads, unemployment rates, intelligence indicators, narcotics use, and arrest records. From this data Moynihan concluded that during the near-systematic destruction of the black family by slavery and the nearly ninety years of

Jim Crow segregation, the black family was forced to reconstruct itself on a different basis from whites. According to Moynihan, the African-American male, denied his place as the provider and protector of the family, had abdicated his dominant role to the female. From this analysis Moynihan determined that all but a minority of black families were distorted, in that they failed to form two-parent families and lacked strong, positive role models for young black men.

Moynihan deliberately avoided making specific policy recommendations in his report, feeling it would distract policymakers from focusing on the major problem. But the policy implications were clear: specific programs were to promote the establishment of a stable, male-dominant family structure. In a memorandum to President Johnson, he outlined several policies that he thought would strengthen this goal. Among them were jobs, especially for black males, decent family housing, and birth control.[16]

Johnson's use of Moynihan's (still confidential) thesis in a speech at a Howard University commencement in 1965 precipitated one of the most controversial eras in public policy debate. News reports of *The Negro Family* made their way into public discourse. These reports emphasized the lurid details of black ghetto "pathology," and minimized the historic background context of institutional racism.

Historians and social scientists criticized Moynihan for faulty use of history and statistics. Moynihan's major thesis, that slavery had historically deformed the black family, was disputed by historian Herbert Gutman: "Moynihan ... [had] confused the problems of poor blacks in the second half of the twentieth century with those of their great-grandparents in the first half of the nineteenth. And he misperceived the history of both groups," mistaking class characteristics for racial ones. Gutman speculated that the breakdown of the black family in the later part of the twentieth century may have been due to the massive "enclosure" movement between 1940 and 1970 that displaced blacks from their land in the rural South and threw them into conditions of chronic unemployment and underemployment, made worse by continuing institutional racism and restrictive welfare regulations.[17] Anthropologist Carol Stack showed that even in very poor welfare-dependent black communities, extensive networks of kin and non-kin substitutes enabled black families to survive amidst formidable odds.[18]

The comments of civil rights leader James Farmer summarized the depth of the feelings of outrage and betrayal brought on by Moynihan's *Report:*

> By laying the primary blame for present-day inequalities on the pathological condition of the Negro family and community, Moynihan has provided a massive academic cop-out for the white conscience and clearly implied that Negroes in this nation will never secure a substantial measure of freedom until we learn to behave ourselves and stop buying Cadillacs instead of bread.... This well-enough intentioned analysis provides the fuel for a new racism... it succeeds in taking the real tragedy of black poverty and serving it up as an essentially salacious "discovery" suggesting that Negro mental health should be the first order of business in a civil rights revolution.[19]

Oscar Lewis, as noted earlier, had attributed the origins of the culture of poverty to the social, economic, and political relations of capitalist societies. He had suggested a policy response that in effect was a call to class struggle. Moynihan's thesis, for all its implications of "blaming the victim," still looked to liberal solutions: providing jobs and family support to the poor. But the culture of poverty thesis was quickly adapted to the agendas of those who wanted to end poverty programs altogether.

Edward Banfield, unlike Lewis and Moynihan, denied any causal link between the culture of poverty and socioeconomic conditions. Indeed, Banfield refused to recognize that long-standing poverty even existed in the contemporary United States. Extreme destitution, he argued, was simply a fleeting condition, experienced by those who suffered some sudden reversal of fortune, such as a layoff or the death of a breadwinner. These conditions could easily be reversed and the victim would no longer be poor.[20] For Banfield, such people were the "deserving poor," since their poverty came about through no fault of their own. Others, for whom poverty was not a temporary condition, he labeled members of the "lower class." This kind of poverty had "as its proximate... cause ways of thinking and behaving that are, in the adult, if not elements built into personality, at least more or less deeply ingrained habits."[21]

In Banfield's lower class, impulsive and often violent behavior, sexual promiscuity, and detachment from family and community were all common traits, consequences of what he called "extreme present-orientation."

> The lower class person lives from moment to moment, he is either unable or unwilling to take account of the future or to control his impulses. Improvidence and irresponsibility are direct consequences of this failure to take the future into account ... and these consequences have further consequences: being improvident and irresponsible, he is also likely to be unskilled, to move frequently from one dead-end job to another, to be a poor husband and father....[22]

Banfield's thesis rested on his own division of U.S. society into four classes—the lower class, the working class, the middle class, and the upper class—whose positions in society were set not by how they drew income or their role in the workforce, but by each class's *orientation to time.* The lower class, Banfield's argument, was most present-time oriented, while the upper class was most oriented to the future. By extension, the upper class were deserving of their wealth and most capable of leading the community, the nation, and the world.[23] Banfield implied that movement up the class ladder was almost an automatic function of the passage of time, and that each immigrant group, as it entered U.S. society from a position in the lower class, moved up the hierarchy.

Banfield linked present-time orientation to rural, "backward" thinking. Though his work dealt with urban poverty, he asserted that this culture did not originate in the city but was imported by poor rural emigrants. Since African-Americans were the last major group to emigrate to urban centers, according to Banfield's thesis, their place was in the lower class, though like any other group most could be expected to rise out of it, given enough time. Banfield acknowledged the existence of race prejudice, but argued that its intensity and institutionalization had diminished. As a result, the problems facing the black poor had more to do with class than with race.

Since Banfield assumed the existence of a permanent but fluid class structure he saw no usefulness in policies to eradicate poverty. Most of the programs the government had initiated, he claimed, were ineffective. The only policies that were likely to reform the "lower class" were ones that would try to isolate them as a group and control their behavior, but our constitutional democracy, he admitted, would make such efforts difficult.

BLAMING THE WELFARE STATE

During the 1960s and early 1970s, the culture of poverty thesis pushed liberals toward a "blame-the-victim" approach usually linked with conservatism. A decade later a group of theories appeared that moved the debate farther to the right: the "dysfunctional welfare state" thesis. In these theories the blame is placed on the very programs of the New Deal and the War on Poverty that had attempted to solve the poverty problem.

Writers like George Gilder, Charles Murray, and Lawrence Mead took off from the apparent failure of Johnson's antipoverty programs, while responding to rising public fear over crime and social decay.

From the late 1950s and throughout the 1960s, poverty, as measured by the number of people living below the government's poverty line, had been decreasing. Beginning around 1973, however, the poverty rate began to climb. Conservative theorists like Banfield who had tried to dismiss the existence of widespread destitution lost credibility. The new conservative explanation was presented in George Gilder's book, *Wealth and Poverty*, which made the best-seller list in 1981.[24]

A moralist more than a social scientist, Gilder views the capitalist system as the promise of endless opportunities for those willing to work hard. Gilder attributes poverty to three kinds of failure on the part of poverty's victims: the failure to work hard; the failure of appropriate family modeling (Moynihan's pathology); and the lack of faith: "Faith in man, faith in the future, faith in the rising returns of giving [Gilder's definition of working hard], faith in the mutual benefits of trade, faith in the providence of God..." which "are all essential to successful capitalism."[25]

Like Moynihan, Gilder says the poor are different because they grow up in female-headed families; the lack of appropriate family modeling is the source of the other two failures. But Gilder's thesis rests on a biological theory far removed from Moynihan's socioeconomic frame. Males and females, he argues, differ in their ability to make use of the opportunity for hard work that capitalism provides. Men's innate aggressive sexual drives motivate them to work hard, but only if they are channeled through monogamous patriarchal marriage. If not, they are dissipated in impulsive, present-oriented behavior—exactly the kind of behavior Banfield attributed to the "lower class." "What Banfield is describing," says Gilder, "... is largely the temperament of single, divorced and separated men." Women, on the other hand, because they are the childbearers, are oriented toward the future. However, distracted by family care and other concerns, they tend not to make earning money a top priority in their lives. Thus, those most likely to succeed in a capitalist society are married, monogamous men who can devote long hours to hard work.[26]

In short, poverty results in a high number of unattached males and female-headed families in low-income communities. This, in turn, leads to more poverty. Without monogamous, patriarchal family models, young men have little motivation to work, save, and believe in the future.

This deviant family structure is created and perpetuated by the welfare state. By replacing the role of male provider with the government, the welfare system robs men of the diligence and discipline needed to succeed in a capitalist system.

Only the men can usually fight poverty by working, and all the antipoverty programs—to the extent they make the mother's situation better—tend to make the father's situation worse; they tend to reduce his redemptive need to pursue the longer horizons of his career.[27]

Dismissing racial and gender discrimination as possible sources of poverty, Gilder not only attacks the most visible welfare program (Aid to Families With Dependent Children), but the entire apparatus of the welfare state.

Unemployment compensation promotes unemployment.... Disability insurance in all its multiple forms encourages the promotion of small ills into temporary disabilities and partial disabilities into total and permanent ones. Social security payments may discourage concern for the aged and dissolve the links between generations.... Comprehensive Employment and Training (CETA) subsidies for government make-work may enhance a feeling of dependence on the state without giving the sometimes bracing experience of genuine work.[28]

This analysis leads Gilder to conclude that the welfare state should be reduced and made unattractive and "even a bit demeaning."[29] The goal of welfare programs should be to help people out of dire but temporary downturns in fortune. "A sensible program would be relatively easy on applicants in emergencies but hard on clients who overstay their welcome."[30] A minimal, temporary welfare program, he suggests, should be supplemented with a universal system of taxable child allowances such as those in most European countries. His goal is not lifting the burden of suffering for children but making it easier for men to take their rightful place as family head. The assumption that women choose single parenthood so they can get welfare is taken as a given by Gilder.

Dismissing any thought of redistributing the wealth downward as a solution to poverty (for example, through a more progressive tax system), Gilder suggests that the most effective way to deal with poverty is to increase the rate of investment by reducing taxes on the rich, the famous "trickle-down" theory. On paper, as the economy grows, economic benefits will "trickle down" to the poor through an increase in the number of jobs. He admits that doing this will increase inequality. Anything less, however, will cut productivity, limit job opportunities, and perpetuate poverty by reducing the work incentive of the poor.[31] This policy, in the form of "supply-side economics," was instituted by the Reagan administration and pursued with a vengeance by the Republican-dominated Congress elected in 1994.

Gilder's philosophy of self-reliance was followed by Charles Murray's *Losing Ground: American Social Policy 1950-1980* (1984),[32] which purports to be a scientific study of the relationship between liberal social policy and the growth of poverty. Murray seeks to demonstrate statistically that increasing poverty rates after 1973 coincided with three types of events which logically should have reduced poverty: (1) the most dramatic rise in government spending for programs targeted at the poor since the Great Depression; (2) a host of liberal legislation, court decisions, and changes in administrative policy (for example, affirmative action programs) that made it easier for the poor to get government benefits; and (3) a growth in the gross national product that Murray claims was actually greater than during the 1950s when the poverty rate was declining. If the poor were growing more numerous and antisocial after all this government help, Murray concludes, the antipoverty programs must not be working.

Murray goes further, however, to assert that the programs were actually the *cause* of deepening poverty. His conclusion is based upon the belief that people are essentially lazy and amoral and will not work to improve their condition unless coerced into doing so. By making it too easy to collect government benefits, liberal social policy had made it profitable, and rational, for the poor to be lazy and degenerate. From this consideration, Murray calls for the entire structure of social welfare legislation, with the exception of unemployment insurance, to be scrapped and every court decision favoring affirmative action to be reversed.

What would people do without such minimal kinds of support as welfare, food stamps, worker's compensation, Medicaid, and subsidized housing? Murray's answer: private charity and local tax-supported services, but only for the "deserving poor." For the rest, it is simply sink or swim.

> Billions for equal opportunity, not one cent for equal outcome— such is the slogan to inscribe on the banner of whatever cause my proposals constitute.... Some people are better than others. They deserve more of society's rewards, of which money is only one small part.... Government cannot identify the worthy, but it can protect a society in which the worthy can identify themselves.... I am proposing a triage of a sort, triage by self-selection.[33]

Murray's book, like the Moynihan Report fifteen years earlier, elicited a flurry of criticism that his reasoning and analysis of quantitative data was flawed and his prescriptions heartless and cruel.[34] Nevertheless, his analysis and prescription found a warm reception in the Reagan White House. In fact, *Losing Ground* was often cited as the Reagan administration's bible.[35]

Even though most conservatives agreed with Murray's criticisms of the welfare system, few were willing to go quite as far as his prescription suggested before 1994. Sophisticated conservatives, according to Katz,

> know the inevitability of big government in modern America. Their problem is to make it work for their ends and to set it on a plausible theoretical and moral base. This was the task begun by Lawrence Mead....[36]

Mead, a New York University political scientist and the author of *Beyond Entitlement: The Social Obligations of Citizenship* (1986), starts out with low expectations of human nature. "Civility," he says, while essential to humane society, "is not a natural condition, as Americans tend to assume. It is something societies must achieve, in part through public authority."[37]

For Mead, the most important function of government is not the protection of civil rights and liberties, the raising of living standards, or the enhancement of democratic participation, but the creation and maintenance of order. Alarmed by what he perceives as a deterioration of social responsibility, especially among the poor (as reflected in crime rates and out-of-wedlock births) and in school and work-related competencies (as reflected in declining SAT scores and unemployment rates), he argues that the liberal welfare state is not necessarily too big, it is simply too permissive.

> ... [Federal programs for the poor] have given benefits to their recipients but have set few requirements for how they ought to function in return. In particular, the programs have as yet no serious requirements that employable recipients work in return for support. There is good reason to think that recipients subject to such requirements would function better.[38]

In order to arrive at this conclusion, Mead has to dismiss the impact of larger social forces on poverty. Today's social problems, he asserts, are not generally due to oppression, and unemployment is not due to a lack of jobs.

> For both rich and poor alike, work has become increasingly elective, and unemployment voluntary, because workers commonly have other sources of income, among them government programs. Jobseekers are seldom kept out of work for long by a literal lack of jobs. More often, they decline the available jobs as unsatisfactory, because of unrewarding pay and conditions.[39]

Voluntary unemployment is only a problem for society, however, when it afflicts the poor. Mead's solution is to require the poor to work off their welfare checks.

> Low-wage work apparently must be mandated, just as a draft has sometimes been necessary to staff the military. Authority achieves compliance more efficiently than benefits, at least from society's viewpoint.[40]

Such programs would apply to mothers with children over the age of three who would have to find their own day care. Their work would not necessarily have to be well-paying or even rewarding. Noncompliance would result in denial of assistance to the entire family and could possibly be a grave act against the state, like the refusal to be drafted. Mead's call for an enhanced state in coercing the poor to behave does not, however, call for an enhanced state to assure that there are jobs available. The welfare state becomes a channeling agency forcing recipients to choose between near-slavery and possible imprisonment—with neither choice offering a way out of poverty.

JUST PLAIN INFERIOR

After the fall of Nazi Germany, which exposed the brutality of the doctrine of racial superiority, poverty theorists have backed away from social Darwinist theories ("survival of the fittest") that were in vogue in the late nineteenth century.[41] Though some academics had revived the discussion in recent years, they were largely dismissed by the mainstream social scientific community and their works received little or no attention outside of narrow scholarly circles.

In 1994, however, Charles Murray and the late Richard Herrnstein, a Harvard psychologist, resurrected the genetic argument in their book *The Bell Curve*, which shortly became a bestseller and turned Murray into a talk show celebrity. The book's publication also generated the fiercest debate among social scientists since reports of Moynihan's *The Negro Family* were leaked to the press in 1965.

The Bell Curve purports to be a scientific demonstration of the relationship between class, genes, and intelligence. Murray and Herrnstein argue that there is an underlying core of intelligence that can be measured by I.Q. tests whose results offer a fairly accurate predictor of socioeconomic status. Those testing high tend to be better off; middle is dumb and poor is dumber.

Murray and Herrnstein argue that as unemployed men and welfare mothers proliferate and pass on their genes to their children, they create an unruly, violent underclass that no government programs or remedial education will be able to help. By the same token, an affluent, well-educated elite passes on a genetic heritage of high culture and civilization to their offspring. As the gap widens between the mental haves and have-nots, the authors predict the rise of a new kind of social polarization in which the haves will increasingly employ the apparatus of a repressive police state to protect themselves from the underclass, much as the affluent do in Latin America.

Citing statistics that show that the average African-American I.Q. score is fifteen points lower than whites' and that disproportionate numbers of African-Americans live in poverty, *The Bell Curve* makes connections between race, intelligence, and behavior that echo those of the social Darwinists and Nazis.

The parallels are not exaggerated. When economic success and failure are thought to be inherited, the most hostile prejudices in a society are unleashed. With public acceptance and influence on policy makers, the genetic thesis would legitimize public antagonism toward the African-American poor and result in punitive, and even genocidal, policies. After all, it was not so long ago that similar theses were used as the rationale leading to slavery, sterilization, and mass human extermination both here and abroad.

Murray and Herrnstein themselves cautioned that their book, "wrongly construed, might do harm." As one reviewer noted, their thesis "may be saying with scientific references and assurances of [Murray's] own good will what others murmur darkly in barrooms and taxis."[42]

IT'S THE ECONOMY

In a series of articles in *The New Yorker* in 1981, journalist Ken Auletta coined a new term: "the underclass."[43] As described by Auletta and repeated in hundreds of different ways in more scholarly language, the underclass is said to consist of hostile street and career criminals, hustlers, those dependent on welfare, and "the traumatized": homeless alcoholics, drug addicts, and the mentally.[44]

The underclass perspective assumes that a new class of hardcore poor has emerged as poverty has become more concentrated and more intractable. In this sense, the underclass is a modern version of the "undeserving poor." Other theorists and historians, however, have disputed the use of the term as poor social science and disguised racism. It narrows the focus for research on poverty, they assert, and leads to short-sighted and misleading conclusions.[45]

Historian Jacqueline Jones refutes the assumption that a marginalized underclass is something new in U.S. history. She points out that today's marginalized poor are much more geographically and racially diverse than they are being depicted by the majority of underclass researchers.[46]

William Julius Wilson, a University of Chicago sociologist, uses the term in a more scholarly sense. In *The Truly Disadvantaged* (1987)[47] and other writings, Wilson argues that a qualitative change in inner-city poverty occurred between the 1960s and the 1980s. It became more concentrated, with more welfare dependency, more unemployment, more antisocial overtones, and more single-parent families.

Wilson points to a "ghetto culture" generated by the social isolation and powerlessness of the inner-city poor, but not a "culture of poverty" in the conservative sense.[48] The underclass described by Wilson is not rooted in the welfare state, but in intensified conditions of urban crisis.

For Wilson, "the rise and fate of the underclass—and hence the efficacy and need for welfare—are inextricably connected to the structure and performance of the American economy."[49] Drawing on economic and census data, he seeks to explain why unemployment has increased among African-American men in the central cities. He traces this to structural shifts in the labor market.

The domestic shutting down of industries has reduced manufacturing jobs that unskilled or semiskilled black men once depended on for a steady living and substituted low-wage service jobs. Because inner-city blacks were disproportionately located in the manufacturing sector, the loss of these jobs has been particularly severe for them. Meanwhile, single parenthood has increased because the lack of male jobs makes marriage less attractive.

Black women generally, but especially young black females residing in large cities, are facing a shrinking pool of "marriageable" (that is, economically secure) men.... Other things being equal, a minimal pool of securely employed males is a necessity, if not a sufficient, condition for the smooth functioning of a stable marriage market.[50]

STILL LEFT BEHIND

Milwaukee has pulled itself out of a serious slump in the early 1980's and staved off the current recession by making its old manufacturing plants more efficient and expanding services like hotels and retailing.... But that strategy has had an unintended but equally profound secondary effect. It has devastated the city's poor black neighborhoods, whose residents thrived in the high-wage union jobs of the city's manufacturing heyday and are now adrift on a rising tide of unemployment, crime and despair.

With black joblessness five times the rate among whites, "Milwaukee is a classic case of how a restructured economy has diminished the employment opportunities for blacks and for black males in particular," said Dr. James H. Johnson Jr., director of the Center for the Study of Urban Poverty at the University of California at Los Angeles, who has studied poverty in Milwaukee.... The result is a city of 628,000 people where black men stand idle on street corners just blocks from the breweries and factories that used to employ them, while well-dressed white-collar workers sell insurance or computers out of some of those same factories, now converted into office parks.—*New York Times*[51]

As industries abandon urban areas, the population of cities themselves have changed. Middle-class and stable working-class families—black as well as white—are leaving cities. The effect on the inner-city poor is devastating:

> The absence of stable working families makes it considerably more difficult to sustain basic institutions in the inner city, for it cuts deep into their membership and saps their base of support.... The decline of these organizations, in turn, weakens means of formal and informal social control and contributes to increasing levels of crime and street violence, which helps accelerate the deterioration of the neighborhood.[52]

Wilson offers important contributions on the role of neighborhoods in the social isolation of today's inner-city poor. With the loss of middle class institutions, employment channels disappear and schools deteriorate. Since most of the new jobs paying more than a minimum wage require more education than the manufacturing jobs that were lost, the deterioration of inner-city schools places poor blacks at an even greater disadvantage in the labor market. Massive public housing projects placed in the most devastated parts of the city concentrate poverty further.[53]

Wilson concludes that the only solution to black poverty is "a comprehensive social-democratic agenda of reform"—a program of full employment, a rise in the minimum wage, more job training, subsidized child care for working mothers, and universal social insurance programs as in Sweden.[54] (Such programs, described in Chapter 5, are exactly what conservatives seek to abolish.)

Labor Secretary Robert Reich also finds the roots of growing poverty in social and economic changes. We are now, says Reich, in an international labor market brought on by advances in telecommunications and transportation. The functions Americans perform within this new integrated global economy will determine their individual fortunes.

> Some Americans, whose contributions to the global economy are more highly valued in world markets, will succeed, while others, whose contributions are deemed far less valuable will fail.... No longer are Americans rising or falling together, as if in one large national boat. We are, increasingly, in different, smaller boats.[55]

According to Reich, 75 percent of the new labor market is composed of three different types of jobs. At the top end, commanding the highest salaries and requiring the most education and training (a college degree or above) are "symbolic analysts," so called because they require "problem-solving, problem-identifying and strategic brokering activities."[56]

In the second group are "routine production workers," including both assembly-line manufacturing jobs and routine office jobs like data processing. Simple computation is the only education required for such jobs. The third category, "in-person service," includes jobs that require little education and some vocational training, and involve public contact—face-to-face services, such as hospital aides or restaurant workers.

Since the first two types of jobs can now be performed anywhere in the world, U.S. workers must compete with workers across the globe. Only the in-person service jobs are stationary. Because routine production jobs are labor-intensive and require minimal education and training, such jobs will flow to where the labor is cheaper. Symbolic analysts' jobs, on the other hand, will flow to where the education, skill, and insights of the workers match the demand for such credentials.

The result of this changed employment landscape is increasing income inequality both here and abroad. In the 1950s and 1960s, says Reich, the economic picture of the American population conformed to the typical bell curve; high in the middle and tapering out gradually at both ends.

> But beginning in the mid-1970s, and accelerating sharply in the 1980s, the crest of the wave began to move toward the poorer end. More Americans were poor. The middle began to sag, as the portion of middle-income Americans dropped. And the end representing the richest Americans began to elongate, as the rich became much richer.[57]

The growth in inequality has been dramatic even among people who hold jobs. There are now more working poor than at any time since World War II. On the other side of the coin, the global mobility of capital has removed the restraints that a national economy once placed on top corporate salaries and other compensation. Unemployment itself is not a significant factor in the growth of poverty, according to Reich: "... [The] truth is that by the last decade of the twentieth century, almost all Americans who wanted to work could find a job.... the more important issue over the longer term is the quality of jobs, not the number."[58]

Reich finds that symbolic analysts—about 20 percent of the voting age population—are increasingly isolated from the rest of society. The trend toward government shrinkage and privatization in contemporary politics reflects this change. Since the only thing that creates community in a global labor market is shared income level, the solution to recovering a sense of national community and political inclusion is to raise the income levels of the lower four-fifths of the population. To do this, Reich would provide every "reasonably talented" child with the opportunity to become a symbolic analyst, which would require large investments in child health and nutrition, in public education from the elementary to the graduate level, and in the info-tech industries that use and generate work in symbolic analysis.[59]

Admitting that many are unlikely to become members of this highly skilled elite, Reich suggests that there are other ways to prepare workers for a more competitive position in the international economy. One is to increase the number of jobs that could apply symbolic analysis to routine production and in-person services. This still might not prevent the drain of routine production jobs to low-wage countries, however, since workers in those countries would also be learning this technology.

Reich seeks to solve the problem of growing domestic and international inequality with the development of a "positive economic nationalism, in which each nation's citizens take primary responsibility for enhancing the capacities of their countrymen for full and productive lives, but who also work with other nations to ensure that these improvements do not come at others' expense."[60]

THE RADICAL CRITIQUES

Since the 1960s, the rise of radical social movements have given rise to equally radical alternatives to official liberal and conservative poverty theories. The feminization of poverty thesis has taken shape out of the work of numerous scholars exploring the role of gender in determining income, wealth, and socioeconomic and political status.[61]

This thesis challenges poverty theorists who view marriage as the way out of poverty for women, and political economists who assume that full employment alone will equalize women's status. A main focus of this feminist approach to women's poverty has been the discriminatory sexual division of labor in both the home and workplace.

Feminists have also demonstrated how females were historically discriminated against by employers, real estate brokers, insurance companies, and unions. State and federal governments refused to recognize and make provisions for family care, such as adequate child care and paid family leave legislation.

Women have also been hampered by a workplace setting and a work pace that assumes that workers do not have family responsibilities that would require them to leave work early, to pick up children from school, or to take days off to care for sick family members. Workers are thus forced to choose between family responsibilities or career advancement, and women have been the losers in this forced choice.

With the decline of two-parent families and of male wages in recent years, more women than ever before have been forced to support their families through wage labor. If employed, single mothers must work a double shift—an unpaid shift in the home and an underpaid shift in the workplace. State welfare programs offer a safety net but no way to climb out of poverty. Cutbacks make it even harder to survive. Such problems are doubled when racial discrimination in hiring, housing, services, and wages are added.[62]

For feminist theorists, the unpaid work women have traditionally done in the home should be recognized as socially useful work that contributes to a nation's gross domestic product. Such work could be compensated through a variety of means: universal child allowances for all families; guaranteed child support from absent parents or through public funds; paid family leaves; universal, subsidized child care; and expansion of the Earned Income Tax Credit.[63]

Beyond such family support, workplace discrimination would be lessened through equal pay for equal work (now mandated by law), by legislation mandating equal pay for work of comparable value, and by enforcement of affirmative action programs.

In the 1960s, a number of African-American scholars and black-power advocates began to criticize the "culture of poverty" thesis. They turned the framework around by rooting black poverty in the subordinate status of the African-American community within the dominant white-controlled society.[64] Historically, African-Americans, always the "last hired and first fired," were excluded from trade unions and apprenticeship programs, given the poorest paying and dirtiest jobs, and were often used as scab labor by employers seeking to break labor militancy in the segregated white workforce. Black communities were subject to segregation, whether *de jure* (legally enforced) or *de facto* (unauthorized, but no less real). They were denied equal educational opportunities, denied credit by banks that took community money and invested it elsewhere, and, until the 1960s, were denied any political power.

The result was a black community that was unable to generate its own capital and thus remained dependent on outside (white) money and white political power for the meager resources doled out to it.

Even after African-Americans had won mayoral elections in many of the nation's largest cities in the 1970s and 1980s, they were unable to govern effectively. The financial base had been drained from the central cities by the flight of middle-class people and jobs to the suburbs. Black elected officials, no less than white ones, sought to lure back white-owned businesses with large tax abatements and other financial favors that further drain cities of the revenues needed to meet the needs of their impoverished residents.

Some contemporary black colony theorists emphasize the need for African-Americans to work toward a transformation of U.S. society in coalition with other groups.[65] Others are pessimistic about the possibilities of converting white America and envision African-Americans separating from white society in order to develop their own institutions and capital base.

All radical theses on poverty draw on the theories that stem from the Marxist tradition. According to classical Marxism, inequality has been present in most societies throughout history, but the capitalist system generates its own particular form of inequality. That is, the existence of poverty and inequality is rooted in the "logic of capitalism." This inequality appears in the form of an unequal relationship between workers (everyone who must "sell" their labor power to another in order to survive) and capitalists (those who own the means of production and control the workers' means of survival).

Some Marxists argue that no adequate solution to poverty is possible within the capitalist system. Others maintain that extreme poverty can be moderated through a welfare state that uses the tax system to redistribute wealth from those at the top to the working class and the vulnerable. Then, working with capitalists and labor, the state would be enabled to anticipate and plan for structural changes in the economy. The full employment policies pursued by the social democratic governments in Sweden are the best examples of this type of approach.[66]

All poverty theories should be open to question. Without practical application, they may have meaning but very little importance. Like any theory, they must hold up against empirical testing of their hypotheses, as well as to examination of their logic.

Naturally, the researcher's own nontestable assumptions, values, or articles of faith, determine which factors will be emphasized when the theory becomes policy. So to understand the practical implications of a theory, it's important to identify the human beings and situations behind the abstractions.

Poverty theory has not existed in a vacuum, nor has it been limited to the ivory towers of higher education. The think tanks, the research projects, and the study groups that produce the theories are funded, housed, and publicized, not for the cause of pure knowledge, but for political purposes. The application of theory as policy, as we will see in the next chapter, has in turn affected the course of politics in dramatic ways.

4

FROM POLICY TO PRACTICE

According to a recent study of seven industrialized countries, the United States ranked first in overall household and child poverty. Its child poverty rate was nearly twice as high as the overall average. In absolute terms, its poor were poorer than those on the bottom in most of Europe. The main feature that separates our country from the others is the limited nature of our welfare state—dramatically less generous than the other countries', by any measure.[1]

Compared with Canada and most European democracies, the United States not only provides the least public support to its citizens, but historically has been the last to offer such support. Germany's chancellor Otto von Bismarck first introduced social security legislation in the 1880s. Great Britain's National Insurance Act was passed in 1911, providing unemployment insurance. During the 1920s, national social security plans were developed in many other European countries, in some Latin American nations, and in Japan. By the end of the 1930s, Sweden had established health and unemployment insurance for wage earners, along with housing subsidies, old age pensions, and paid vacations and maternity leaves.[2]

Over and over, when confronted with the realities of poverty, unemployment, and other kinds of economic suffering, U.S. policymakers have left it to the market to redistribute the benefits of economic growth. This chapter will explore the basis for this quirk, in the context of the history of poverty policy since the Great Depression.

THE WELFARE STATE

First coined by Archbishop William Temple in *Citizen and Churchmen*, 1941, the "welfare state" refers to the array of programs and policies that many governments undertake to reduce the inequalities generated by the market, to provide a minimum income floor under all their citizens, to enable their populations to weather such "social contingencies" as sickness, old age and unemployment, and to ensure that everyone, without regard to income, is offered the best standards available in relation to an agreed upon range of social services.—*Charles I. Schottland*[3]

ECONOMIC POLICY IN CONTEXT

There are ideological and political constraints on the work of U.S. policymakers. They work in a political culture that stresses limited government, the "free market," rugged individualism, and (in principle at least) equal opportunity. All these features are connected to a peculiarly Puritan belief that our national culture and our political system are morally superior to and more inventive than other systems and cultures.[4]

Our national creed of combining limited government with a free market (in which fair distribution of resources is a given) comes from the writings of the British and Scottish philosophers

John Locke and Adam Smith, and from the original American colonists' yearning for political and economic independence. Through the years this basic notion has kept large sections of the public resistant to the idea of a labor or socialist government. After the experience of the British monarchy's heavy hand, the property-owning founding fathers left a legacy of thinking that views socialism, welfare, and even public education and health as "foreign."

Once a liberating concept, the ever-present individualism in U.S. culture—the idea that we are "heroic architects of our own individual fates"[5]—has undermined the solidarity among working people common to most industrialized societies. There is no longer a sense of a shared "public good."[6] For many, the very idea of state action aimed at promoting that public good is seen as an intrusion and even a threat to individual liberty.[7] By the same standard, "equal opportunity" without a commitment to equality of results has spread misconceptions about who is hit by poverty and discrimination, and why.

The clash between myth and reality goes all the way to the historic bedrock. The United States, as "sweet land of liberty" and world savior, has an ugly side: the genocide of Native Americans, slavery, the massive exploitation here and around the world by the industrial juggernaut, and the U.S. government's repression of human rights in the service of a "stable business climate" for the corporate sector.

On the political side, public policy is deeply affected by class bias in the structure of the system itself. As discussed in Chapter 1, the founding fathers were well aware—even in 1781—of conflicting political interests based on class differences. They sought to prevent the political dominance of those who "labor under all the hardships of life and secretly sigh for a more equal distribution of its blessings"—that is, wage earners, the propertyless, the working majority.

The framers' answer was to construct a "republican" form of government, which by today's standards was anything but democratic. A republican government, as James Madison explained in *The Federalist Papers*, was designed to have as few people as possible represent the interests of the many. In this way the "leveling spirit" so feared by the framers could be kept from influencing the political agenda.[8] Using a purposely obscure political device for electing presidents (the electoral college) as well as single-member voting districts, winner-take-all rules for counting votes, a Senate that was elected by state legislatures until 1913, and property-, race-, and gender-based restrictions on voting, the founding fathers succeeded in keeping voting rights from the majority for more than 130 years.

When an industrial working class arose in the latter half of the nineteenth century, a two-party structure, based on ethnic, religious, and regional interests rather than on class, was already firmly entrenched (whereas openly class-based parties were standard in European systems). The rules governing this party system made it extremely difficult, if not impossible, for third parties representing alternative ideologies and interests to gain ballot access. Populist movements' attempts to rally for Democrats in order to challenge the alliance between big business and the Republican Party were been repeatedly turned back by entrenched capital.[9] The corporate-Republican alliance maintained its dominance in national life until the election of 1932.

Within their republican model, the founders constructed the federalist system, which divided power between the national, state, and lower levels of government in ways that often overlap and conflict. Reforms are hard to put in place and, once established, hard to change. A complex arrangement of constituencies, staggered electoral cycles, differing state election rules, a system of checks and balances at the federal and state levels, etc., combine to discourage the rise of a politically motivated majority. Only well-funded elites have the time, the resources, and the expertise to negotiate such a system. Over the years, this advantage has alienated large segments of eligible voters, even as formal barriers to universal voting rights have been removed.

The last and deepest roadblock to challenging poverty is the enduring legacy of slavery. Just how the unpaid labor of African-

Americans helped to create the capital needed to trigger an industrial revolution is not taught and rarely understood. The wedge between higher and lower, skilled and unskilled, has been racialized in our country—so much so that notions of a self-interested working class, so common in other countries, are undermined by our infamous "color line." Instead, the myth of the lazy black and brown population who take and give nothing back is passed along in innumerable forms, including folk tales, jokes, cartoons, movies, and even history textbooks.

In these ways the system, in particular its racist aspect, has kept most people in the United States relatively uninterested in politics. Without a working-class majority aware of its exploited position and potential to transform its condition through organization, a full-fledged welfare state never had a chance—even during the Great Depression.

THE NEW DEAL

Until the 1930s, the federal government offered no social safety net for the poor. Aid had always been needed—our history is one long series of recurrent, severe recessions. Assistance was largely directed towards the "deserving poor"—white women, the disabled, and the elderly—and came from two main sources: private charities and local government.

During the Depression, the near collapse of the economy, the general suffering caused by economic hardship, and the failure of laissez-faire policies to regenerate growth led to widespread demands for government intervention. But the government did not respond until social unrest produced a massive electoral shift to the Democrats under Franklin D. Roosevelt.[10]

THE COLLAPSE

> By the time FDR took office, voluntary agencies had exhausted their human and financial resources, and states and cities, teetering on the edge of bankruptcy, clamored for federal aid. Across the country, unemployed workers agitated for more relief, staged rent strikes, and rioted for food, and, not long after FDR's election, the Townsendites, Huey Long's share-the-wealth movement, and demagogues like Father Coughlin galvanized their followers into social movements that demanded quick, simple, sometimes frightening, solutions to the social and economic crisis.—*Michael B. Katz*[11]

President Roosevelt's New Deal can be divided into two phases. During the first phase, from 1933 to early 1935, the government responded to the deepening crisis with test programs aimed at making market forces act more constructively in response to widespread unemployment. Since the country had never faced a crisis quite as severe, the field was wide open.

By 1933, the thinking of British economist John Maynard Keynes was gaining influence among U.S. economists.[12] Keynes argued that active government intervention in the economy could stabilize business boom-to-bust cycles.

But the early New Deal was firmly rooted in the traditional belief that recovery would come with the revival of private investment. Roosevelt came to office not as a radical reformer but as a fine-tuner for the system with his background in "old money." As governor of New York State, his approach favored the use of government to bring better business planning and coordination. Deficit spending was to be only a temporary tactic.[13] Even at the height of the Depression, government spending was never more than 5.9 percent of the GNP.[14] In contrast, Sweden's Social Democratic government brought in Keynesian policies years earlier and emerged from the Depression before most other countries.[15]

Roosevelt had to appease both a reluctant and sometimes hostile business establishment and an increasingly angry and militant public. But he was unwilling to tamper with the fundamental structures of capitalism. His programs during his first hundred days aimed at stabilizing the economy and putting the unemployed to work.[16]

MAJOR PROGRAMS OF THE "FIRST" NEW DEAL

National Recovery Administration sought business help in stabilizing production, wages, and employment, and granted workers the right to bargain collectively.

Agricultural Adjustment Administration increased farm income by paying farmers not to grow crops (thus limiting supply), provided new institutions of farm credit, federal crop insurance, and special help for disadvantaged farmers.

Public Works Administration loaned money to state and local governments to contract with private firms to hire workers for infrastructure and beautification projects.

Tennessee Valley Authority set up a public corporation to construct dams for flood control and electric generation, to manufacture fertilizer, and to build a model city.

Civilian Conservation Corps provided work for young men in maintaining the national forests.

National Employment Service worked with states to provide a job clearinghouse.

Federal Emergency Relief Administration provided grants-in-aid to states and local agencies for work relief and some direct relief for indigent persons.

Civil Works Administration provided temporary jobs for more than four million people.

In addition to creating job and relief programs, the New Dealers also established the Federal Housing Administration to ensure loans for the building and renovation of private homes, and a variety of administrative and legal safeguards to stabilize the banking and securities industries.

Although the early New Deal programs changed the accepted role of government, they were, at best, experimental. Millions of people were given jobs or relief, but the programs came nowhere near bringing the country out of the Depression; and in several ways they either carried over old problems or created new ones.

For one thing, the jobs programs provided work to only a fraction of the unemployed. Roosevelt's Civilian Conservation Corps, for example, employed only 300,000 to 500,000 each month. While 11 million applied for jobs through the Civil Works Administration (described as the "greatest public works experiment in American history"),[17] only 4 million could get them and the jobs themselves were only temporary.[18] When the Public Works Administration failed to specify that only the jobless should be hired, the result was the employment of already employed skilled workers.[19] In the spring of 1934, one fourth of the labor force was still out of work.[20]

The New Deal also carried over the old racial and gender biases. Jobs under the PWA, CCC, and TVA invariably went to white men; women were entirely excluded and men of color limited to a 10 percent quota.[21] In the FERA, women and African-Americans usually received lower wages than white men.[22] Some policies actually made people poorer. For example, when the AAA took land out of cultivation it displaced many tenant farmers and sharecroppers.[23]

Business was dead set against Roosevelt's work and relief programs, which they attacked as "make-work" and "boondoggles." Their influence kept wages for government jobs programs below the going market rate, to avoid driving wages up in private industry. Despite the minimum wage set by the federal government, many workers under the FERA and in private industry took home wages so low that they had to go on relief.[24]

By early 1935, business opposition to both direct relief payments and jobs programs had grown from a grumble to a roar. Alarmed by an outbreak of strikes in 1933 and 1934, business leaders moved against the growing labor movement. Section 7a of the National Industrial Recovery Act, which gave bargaining power to workers, became a major target. Businesses began forming company (in-house and management-controlled) unions. They were also angered by stock exchange and banking regulations, including the establishment in 1934 of the Securities and Exchange Commission. In the fall of that year, prominent industrial leaders formed the American Liberty League to fight "radicalism" and protect property rights.[25]

Despite this opposition, the Democrats increased their hold on Congress in 1934; but the business attacks had taken their toll. By the spring of 1935, many of the New Deal's most innovative programs were cut or deactivated.[26] In May 1935, the conservative Supreme Court ruled the NRA unconstitutional, a signal that the New Deal might be a goner before it could even show real results.

But the crisis had gone too far. As the Depression dragged on, the public clamored for relief. Proponents of radical reform, including socialists and communists, were gaining converts, and it seemed possible that a left-leaning third party might form in time for the 1936 election.[27]

THE SAFETY NET

Beginning in the summer of 1934, a new approach to relief policy began to take shape within the administration and among prominent Democratic members of Congress. In 1935 and 1937, Frances Perkins, then secretary of labor and head of Roosevelt's Committee on Economic Security, pushed through the passage of four major pieces of legislation that would shape the nation's future. These were the Social Security Act, the Works Progress Administration, the National Labor Relations Act, and the Fair Labor Standards Act. With the passage of the Social Security Act, a compulsory, permanent, federally-run program, to provide old age, survivors', and disability benefits was set up.[28] Other programs, mandated and funded by the federal government but administered by the states, included an unemployment insurance program, income support for poor children (Aid to Dependent Children), Old Age Assistance for those failing to qualify for Social Security, and Aid to the Blind.

These reforms went beyond all previous measures; the nation's understanding of poverty was turning a corner.[29] As noted, the New Deal was first introduced as a set of temporary measures designed to stimulate economic recovery until the private economy kicked in. The Social Security Act was, in effect, a recognition that the economy would *not* bring prosperity. It signalled acceptance of some basic form of insurance for people who would otherwise be left destitute by old age, death, disability, or involuntary unemployment. As Senator Patrick Harrison, the bill's sponsor, put it:

> It [the Social Security Act] is not intended as emergency legislation to cope with an emergency situation, but rather it is designed as a well-rounded program of attack on the principal causes of insecurity which existed prior to the depression and which we may expect to continue in the years to come.[30]

In signing the bill, Roosevelt asserted that it was "only a cornerstone in a structure which is being built but is by no means complete."[31]

The Social Security Act established two different types of programs. The first, called social insurance and politically the most popular, relies on contributions made by employees and employers through a payroll tax.[32] Benefits go to those who have contributed to the program, which includes people at all income levels. Such monies are seen as "earned rights" to be used in necessary cases, such as old age, disability, or involuntary unemployment.

The second set of programs, known as public assistance, provide money, goods, or services from general revenues to people who have not directly contributed to them. To collect such benefits, the recipients must pass a means test; that is, they must show proof that their income is sufficiently low and that their cases fit particular categories of need. Aid to Dependent Children (known more recently as Aid to Families With Dependent Children or AFDC) was originally designated as a small program for the support of the "deserving poor"—the dependent children of widows, who were not expected to be in the workforce. Over the years, however, AFDC—commonly known as "welfare"—came to be seen as a kind of economic narcotic, an unearned handout collected by undeserving single mothers who, legend has it, preferred a government check to an "honest" living.

THE SOCIAL SECURITY PROGRAMS IN 1994

Social insurance programs include *Social Security* (old age, survivors', and disability Insurance); Medicare (old age health insurance); *Unemployment Insurance* (income support for involuntarily unemployed workers); *Veterans Assistance* (various health, educational, income-support, and loan benefits); *Public Employee Retirement;* and *Railroad Retirement.*

Public assistance programs include *Aid to Families With Dependent Children* (cash to meet basic needs, shelter, and heating costs); *Medicaid* (medical insurance for the poor); *Food stamps* (available to low-income individuals and families); *Supplemental Security Income* (for the poor, disabled, and elderly poor, combining three formerly separate programs); *Head Start* (a preschool program for low-income children); Low-income housing and energy subsidies; *Special Supplemental Food Program for Women, Infants, and Children* (nutritional food supplements for low-income mothers and children); School lunch program; College loans and scholarship programs; and *Earned Income Tax Credit* (a tax rebate available to low-income workers with dependent children, administered by the IRS).

Social Security benefits are not strictly tied to earnings. The formula for payment is weighted heavily in favor of low-income workers, assuring them a higher percentage of their preretirement earnings than high-wage workers. It is mildly redistributive in that it transfers money from the wealthy to the lower-income and from the young to the old. Its redistributive nature is limited, since both wealthy and lower-income workers are taxed at the same rate on the same amount of earnings. Thus, the lower- and middle-income groups feel the bite of social insurance taxes more than the rich. With AFDC, the *entire* benefit went to the poor.

Social Security was originally seen as a supplement to the pensions and savings workers would have accrued in the normal course of their working lives. Over the years it has come to be the only source of income for as much as 80 percent of the elderly.[33] As we saw in Chapter 2, between one fifth and one quarter of the elderly would be living below the poverty line without Social Security.

With two distinct channels of benefits, the Social Security Act created the basis for a two-tiered system of social benefits. The results can be seen in the difficulty opponents have in cutting the less redistributive programs, even as they roll right over AFDC.

Roosevelt's next major innovation was the Works Progress Administration (WPA), a temporary work-relief program that was means-tested but less controversial. Three and a half million people who had been receiving direct relief were now to be put to work at a "security wage," higher than what they had been receiving but lower than the prevailing wage in the region in which they were working, and based on skill level. The work produced was to be part of a permanent contribution to the nation, not just "make-work."[34] Before the program ended in 1943, the WPA had given work to more than 8 million people and financial aid to 30 million more. It also produced an infrastructure of public buildings—schools, libraries, hospitals, auditoriums, gymnasiums, etc.; public works—airports, parks and playgrounds, water works and sewage plants, thousands of miles of roads, bridges, drainage ditches and viaducts; and public health projects. The WPA also helped to create artistic and historic legacies—murals, sculptures, and paintings that still adorn public buildings; plays, novels, and poetry that are part of our national heritage; and archival material that has given scholars a better understanding of American history. The WPA succeeded in changing the face of the nation.[35]

However, Roosevelt held back from launching WPA as a permanent standby jobs program, even when his own Committee on Economic Security called for it.[36] The WPA's temporary nature meant that every year Congress had another crack at it through appropriations battles and constant readjustment of its rules. This allowed conservatives to lower its benefits, leaving wages too low to meet people's needs. Wage differentials based on gender, race, and class also persisted.[37] Even at its height, WPA was only able to employ one quarter of the jobless.[38]

Enter the National Labor Relations Act (NLRA, or Wagner Act), passed in 1935, which guaranteed the right of labor to organize and to bargain collectively. The NLRA set up the National Labor Relations Board to serve as a kind of guarantor of justice in labor-management disputes. The Wagner Act significantly altered labor-management relations in the United States, giving labor, for the first time, the legal recognition it had struggled at least ninety years to achieve.

The Fair Labor Standards Act of 1937 established the minimum wage and a maximum work week, and outlawed child labor. With recognition and federal protection, workers were now empowered as never before. From then until 1947, when the management-sponsored Taft-Hartley Act weakened the NLRA, the trade union movement grew from 4 million to 15 million members. But despite this important step in the long fight against poverty, unionized labor has never represented more than a third of the U.S. labor force, compared to almost 90 percent in contemporary Sweden. It is no coincidence that the erosion of the union movement in recent years has been accompanied by deepening poverty and income polarization.

ASSESSING THE NEW DEAL

The programs of the New Deal broke the stranglehold that pro-business theories had exercised over the economy. They also served as social control, and may have saved the capitalist system by offering an alternative to increasingly militant—even revolutionary—labor activity, such as the Flint sit-down strike against General Motors in 1936.[39] The theories and policies proposed by rapidly growing populist movements of the 1930s, like the Townsend Movement, Huey Long's Share Our Wealth movement, and Upton Sinclair's End Poverty in California plan, emphasized the use of federal taxes for redistribution of wealth. Labor was on the march, with impassioned support from the increasingly influential socialists and communists. Comments of administration officials show that they saw their program as a way to head off more radical proposals.[40] For conservatives, on the other hand, the New Deal began the growth of an oppressive big government posing a threat to private enterprise, the spirit of self-reliance, and the work ethic.

There is no doubt that the New Deal represented a break with the past: "The acceptance of Keynesian economic theories," sociologists Sar A. Levitan and Clifford M. Johnson observed, "[...] dispelled the sense of impotence and resignation that had accompanied sharp economic downturns and destroyed the underlying fatalism that business cycles must run their course no matter what their toll in human suffering."[41] In fact, after the New Deal, the idea that government should have the responsibility for relieving human suffering, if not preventing it, became fixed in our national culture. By 1994 it was hard to remember a time when it hadn't been.

Although many were saved from outright starvation, the New Deal policies did not bring us out of the Depression. For one thing, the emergency nature of the crisis, the lack of prior long-term planning, and the early New Deal's flexibility meant that nothing new was really in place until the late 1930s. Even Social Security did not start to pay out benefits until the end of the decade.

Despite its goals of ending the Depression and advancing equality, the New Deal failed in a number of ways. Until 1938 to 1939, when the country was plunged into a depression within the Depression, the Roosevelt administration believed in a philosophy of balanced budgets, with resulting cutbacks in government programs and rises in unemployment whenever there was a hint of economic upturn. Responding to continuing pressure from the business community and the Southern conservative wing of his own party, Roosevelt never allowed New Deal programs to compete with the private sector either in status or wages. The federal system dictated that the powers to run anti-poverty programs be shared with the states; as a result, old-guard racist "Dixiecrats," some with ties to the Ku Klux Klan, gained power to reinforce the inequalities in regional income and poverty described in Chapter 2. The long cycle of depression finally ended as a result of massive government spending in preparation for World War II.

The New Deal did bring an unprecedented expansion of government size and power that would shape the public-private relationship for the rest of the century. Accepted wisdom since then held that the federal government is responsible for setting national standards in everything from wage and income floors to environmental and health and safety regulations. No doubt some of this regulation has been oppressive and overly bureaucratic. Big government, in itself, is not automatically good. But there is also plenty of evidence that without government intervention, the condition of poor and working America would be much worse than it is.

THE FAILED PROMISE OF AMERICAN LIBERALISM

In 1944, amid the horrors brought by fascism and war, Roosevelt set out in his State of the Union address an "Economic Bill of Rights." The proposal was the product of FDR's National Resources Planning Board, which had developed a progressive Keynesian approach to macroeconomic policy. The board had envisioned a postwar economy of full-employment planning, income support, and expanded social programs. It was in the best New Deal tradition.

FDR'S ECONOMIC BILL OF RIGHTS

• The right to a useful and remunerative job in the industries, or shops or farms or mines of the Nation;
The right to earn enough to provide adequate food and clothing and recreation;
• The right of every farmer to raise and sell his products at a return which will give him and his family a decent living;
• The right of every businessman, large and small, to trade in an atmosphere of freedom from unfair competition and domination by monopolies at home or abroad;
• The right of every family to a decent home;
• The right to adequate medical care and the opportunity to achieve and enjoy good health;
• The right to adequate protection from the economic fears of old age, sickness, accident, and unemployment;
• The right to a good education.
• All of these rights spell security. And after this war is won we must be prepared to move forward, in the implementation of these rights, to new goals of human happiness and well-being.[42]

The national mood anticipated more economic equality. Both 1944 presidential candidates called for full employment. Numerous labor and civil rights leaders, veterans, and religious groups, along with the U.S. Conference of Mayors, supported the Economic Bill of Rights. The right to full employment had also been enshrined in the newly passed UN Charter. But it was not to be. The Full Employment Bill of 1945, the first attempt to institute the Economic Bill of Rights, was defeated by House conservatives. Instead of a bill that would have committed the government to a "national policy and program for full employment," the country got the Employment Act of 1946, which said nothing about the right to employment or the government's responsibility to assure it.[43]

With the Depression a fading memory, policymakers were more concerned with consolidating the country's emergence from the war as the predominant economic power. Pent-up consumer demand occasioned by the war, the new markets for American products facilitated by the Marshall Plan, the Interstate Highway Program, and the G.I. Bill pushed aside wartime idealism. The aspiration for equality was not to return for more than a decade.

THE GREAT SOCIETY

In the middle of the cold war, the United States set out to prove that capitalism could solve the country's poverty problem. Staring in the late 1940s, a period of intense competition between the United States and the Soviet Union for scientific and technological hegemony rocked the world. This influenced President Johnson's decision to increase spending for the set of welfare state programs he called "the Great Society." In his 1964 State of the Union address, Lyndon Johnson announced that an "unconditional war on poverty" would be the centerpiece of his administration.

Sociologist Michael B. Katz notes that the choice of military language served several political purposes. It gave Johnson's program the moral appeal of a national security emergency. Second, the public needed a spirit-rallying purpose to counter the mood of shock and despair at the Kennedy assassination. And third, Johnson needed to shed his Southern conservative image in favor of a new, national one.[44] The program that emerged, however, did not live up to Johnson's passionate rhetoric. From the beginning, the War on Poverty, though the largest attempt since the Great Depression to alter the distribution of resources, was limited in conception, scope, administration, and funding.

The Johnson programs drew from two contradictory explanations for poverty. Kennedy-era liberals saw poverty as a result of blocked opportunities. The cause of juvenile delinquency, for example, was seen as "the frustration and rage aroused in poor youngsters by the contrast between the promise and delivery of opportunities."[45] If opportunities could be "unblocked," the poor could compete like everyone else. A major special education program's title, "Head Start," reflected this theory.

As the poverty programs developed, however, conservative theories of cultural deprivation came into play. Now poor people were seen as blocked both by their own lack of cultural skills and the family supports that enabled middle-class people to take advantage of channels for upward mobility. As Katz notes, this theory promoted "equal opportunity" through education, training, and housing programs, rather than job creation.[46] The point was to bring the poor up to the middle-class "starting line" in the race of individuals for upward mobility.[47]

MAJOR EQUAL OPPORTUNITY PROGRAMS OF THE WAR ON POVERTY

Combating juvenile delinquency: *Juvenile Delinquency and Youth Offenses Act*, 1961.

Job preparation and placement: *Manpower Development and Training Act*, 1962 (originally developed for the technologically displaced, expanded and redirected to treat the hard-core unemployed); *Neighborhood Youth Corps* (basic educational and job readiness skills for low-income youth); *Job Corps* (a residential program for ghetto youth, providing basic education, life, and work-readiness skills); *Concentrated Employment Program*, 1967 (block grants to community groups for comprehensive attacks on employment); *Work Incentive Program*, 1967 (training and placement of welfare recipients).

Education: *Operation Head Start* (the most successful and longest lasting of all the programs, providing school-readiness education for disadvantaged children); *Operation Follow Through* (a program to prevent Head Start children from losing their early advantages); *Upward Bound* (preparing bright, poor youth for college); *Higher Education Act*, 1965 (authorized scholarships and low-interest loans for undergraduates and expanded work-study programs); *Open Admissions programs* (a policy to allow college entrance to any high school graduate, to be supplemented with remedial programs while in college).

Expansion of eligibility for existing entitlement programs: A number of executive orders, regulatory changes, and court orders expanded the numbers and types of people who were eligible for government entitlement programs. For example: the *food stamps program*, a small Depression-era project, was expanded and made available to all low-income people within a certain percentage of the poverty line; *Social Security* benefits were increased and indexed to inflation; *Low-income housing subsidies* were increased; *AFDC regulations*, such as year-long waiting periods, were reduced.

Introduction of new programs and services: *Supplemental Security Income* (SSI), 1972 (guaranteed a minimum income to the aged, blind, and disabled poor); *Medicaid*, 1960, and *Medicare*, 1965 (created systems of national health insurance for needy persons and the elderly).

Anti-discrimination legislation and programs: *Civil Rights Act of 1964* (called the most comprehensive piece of civil rights legislation ever passed, bars discrimination on the basis of race, sex, religion, and national origin in almost every area of national life); *Civil Rights Act of 1968* (bars discrimination on the basis of race, religion, sex, or national origin in the advertising, financing, sale, or rental of housing); *Affirmative Action and the Equal Employment Opportunity Commission* (provides and monitors compensatory help for certain classes of people held to be historically the victims of discrimination).

Yet the War on Poverty challenged the racial and political status quo in ways the New Deal never attempted. Johnson responding to mass pressure, built stronger and more aggressive federal agencies, challenging the local political machines that enforced racial discrimination. Unlike FDR, who had worked largely through state and county governments to implement the New Deal programs, the War on Poverty sought to create a direct channel—the Office of Economic Opportunity—between the federal government and the poor. The OEO intervened in local situations where segregation ruled, bypassing state and city governments.[48] Through social service agencies, universities, and new poor people's organizations known as Community Action Programs (CAPs), as well as citywide coordinating agencies, the Johnson administration gave serious attention to the urban poor.[49] It also, mistakenly, thought it could win entrenched state and local political structures to its antipoverty efforts.

CAPs proved to be the most controversial feature of the War on Poverty. When poor people, with the help of federal funds, began to protest racist governing structures in the South and unresponsive city halls in the North, it did not go over well with the traditional political establishment.[50] According to Francis Fox Piven, "local officials were flabbergasted; one level of government and party was financing the harassment of another level of government and party!"[51] Since the 1930s, the power of entrenched political machines that had become typical in large cities and in Southern counties had rested on their control of the flow of federal welfare state dollars. An insurgency from below threatened this political power.

In the program's first year, the mayors of San Francisco and Los Angeles sponsored a resolution at the U.S. Conference of Mayors accusing Sargent Shriver, director of the War on Poverty, of "fostering class struggle."[52] Politicians around the country accused poverty programs of mismanagement and of fomenting violence. They were often successful in holding up the flow of federal funds or of derailing some of the project's most ambitious plans. Congress came under pressure from state and local politicians and later from what many have called a "white backlash"—negative political responses by some working and middle-class whites to the increasingly militant demands of antipoverty activists.[53] Before the end of 1966, Johnson's Office of Economic Opportunity began cutting back on its community action program.

Democratic policymakers laid the groundwork for a schism in the New Deal coalition that would soon bring them defeat. Unwilling to push the private sector by demanding full employment and economic security for everyone, they narrowly targeted inner-city African-Americans and Latinos, even though larger numbers of poor people were white.[54] Conservatives seized the moment. In his 1968 campaign for the presidency, Richard Nixon was able to turn white working- and middle-class voters against the African-American poor and white liberal supporters of antipoverty programs by linking the programs with the urban violence that broke out in over 100 cities in 1967.[55] Welfare mothers were portrayed as undeserving, high-living "welfare queens."[56] Middle-class civil rights and antipoverty supporters were pictured as "knee-jerk liberals" who would support anything, no matter how outrageous, as long as it had to do with blacks. Alternately, they were characterized as "poverty bureaucrats" who were getting rich off their work in the bureaucracies which serviced the poor. So began a long campaign by the pro-business Republican Party to win the support of white working-class voters, by appealing to their fears of black militancy and their rage at "welfare chiselers."

In 1974, less than a decade after it had begun, the War on Poverty was ended—poverty won. When Richard Nixon abolished the Office of Economic Opportunity, the most prominent agency of the War on Poverty, it signaled the end of the government's commitment to eradicating poverty. Community Action and a home-buying aid program were halted altogether. Other programs were either transferred to other agencies or redirected so as not to specifically target the poor.[57]

ASSESSING THE WAR ON POVERTY

Funding for OEO never accounted for more than 3 percent of all federal social welfare expenses or 6 percent of all federal funds for the poor.[58] The great bulk of the social welfare state has always gone to the middle class and an even larger amount—not labeled social welfare—goes into the pockets of the very wealthy, through mortgage deductions, tax shelters, and corporate subsidies. More than anything else, however, it was the Vietnam war that prevented the War on Poverty from coming close to its stated goals. In the heady economic climate of the mid-1960s, Johnson claimed there was enough money for both "guns and butter." But it soon became obvious that pursuing a Vietnam victory would take both years and really big money. Johnson made his choice.

Even so, between 1960 and 1972 the poverty rate was cut in half. The number of elderly living in poverty was reduced dramatically, as Social Security was increased and indexed to inflation. In addition, millions of people gained access to health care through Medicaid and Medicare. Between 1963 and 1970 the number of poor people never examined by a doctor dropped from 20 percent to 8 percent. Between 1965 and 1972 infant mortality dropped by 33 percent. Food stamps and public housing also made some headway.[59] But with the onset of recession and double-digit inflation after 1973, the poverty rate began to climb again.

Critics on the left, like Piven and Richard Cloward, have cited the War on Poverty as another example of the government's use of federal funds to contain social unrest and regulate the labor market.[60] Critics on the right, of course, have used the poverty program as a scapegoat for the seemingly intractable poverty and social pathology they associate with ghetto life. But the Great Society programs could still point to an important breakthrough: the entry they provided into the middle class for millions of African Americans. College programs and federal grants also increased the percentage of black college students, and affirmative action programs enabled white women and racial minorities to get jobs that would otherwise have been closed to them, while narrowing wage differentials.

The Community Action Programs nurtured a form of local politics that opened space for poor communities to claim greater control over the institutions that affected their lives.[61] Organizers from this arena went on in the 1970s and 1980s to lead new movements: tenants' rights, farmworkers' organizing, consumer protection, community economic development, opposition to toxic dumping, nuclear contamination, and plant closings, and more. Legal Services, the legal arm of Community Action, produced a breed of activist lawyers who were successful in using the courts in extending constitutional rights to previously unprotected groups, expanding eligibility criteria for government entitlements, and beginning to define new rights.

FROM NIXON TO REAGAN

Despite this progress, the voices of conservatives claiming government programs to eradicate poverty had done no good—and had actually created greater dependence—got louder. Yet, the welfare state actually *expanded* during the conservative Nixon presidency, with bipartisan congressional support. The welfare state, even in its limited form, had become a fact of government life. People had come to expect and rely on all sorts of social services, and even conservatives saw Keynesian policies more or less as common sense.[62]

The Nixon presidency is best known for two major program innovations in poverty policy: the Family Assistance Act and the Comprehensive Employment and Training Act. The Family Assistance Act, which died in Congress, proposed a guaranteed flat annual income for both the working and non-working poor, with built-in work incentives. A curious alliance of Southern conservatives and welfare mothers helped to defeat it for opposing reasons. Conservatives worried that the bill would undermine low Southern wages, while welfare mothers, who favored the idea, complained that the proposed income was too low to provide the child care, transportation, and other expenses needed to get and hold a job.

The Comprehensive Employment and Training Act (CETA), passed in December 1973, was a response to sharply rising unemployment in the early 1970s. CETA was the first (and last) major job creation program to be undertaken by the federal government since the Great Depression. The program was designed to provide training, work experience, and entry-level public service jobs for the long-term, structurally unemployed. It soon became saddled with two other, somewhat contradictory purposes: to help local communities meet the needs for expanding social services in an era of declining state revenues, and to provide short-term jobs for the recently laid-off.[63]

As a concession to the Nixon administration's "new federalism"—transfering power and decisionmaking back to state and local governments—federal funds were to be given to "prime sponsors" (state and local governments) to design and implement the programs under broad federal guidelines. Allegations of corruption, waste, and nepotism, especially in cities with entrenched political machines, plagued CETA until it was ended by Reagan in 1987. Unfortunately, the program was just beginning to serve the needs and low-income constituencies for which it had been designed.

During the 1970s, business leaders began to regroup politically. The country was growing more hostile and suspicious of the corporate and political "establishment."[64] Meanwhile, business leaders found they had to contend with rising inflation and a rapidly changing, intensely competitive global economy. Their response was dramatic: journalist Thomas Byrne Edsall called it "one of the most remarkable campaigns in the pursuit of political power in recent history."[65] The goal of the private sector was to return U.S. policy to the pre-New Deal days of capitalism unfettered by environmental, health, and safety regulations, redistributive tax policies, and other restrictions on their ability to cut costs and increase profits as they saw fit. The push for a new political climate was made easier by the decline of the old bases of support for the public sector. The labor movement stagnated. The New Deal electoral coalition was breaking apart. The internal political control of parties over candidates and party platforms had changed into media-driven campaign strategies, and new advances in telecommunications technology were re-shaping the electoral process, making it much more difficult to run for office or to win without big money and media appeal.[66]

Public trust in elected officials was at a low point after the disasters of Vietnam and Watergate. But instead of a shift to the left, the new crop of congressional and gubernatorial Democrats and their leader, Jimmy Carter, sounded and acted more like moderate Republicans. The Reagan-era trends in monetary and fiscal policy and in deregulation, including tax cuts for corpo-rations and the wealthy, actually started during the Carter administration.[67]

Meanwhile, corporate money and the religious right began to build an active far-right movement within the Republican Party. Its strategists were bent on paring back the role of the federal government to its bare bones: providing for national defense and domestic social control, and managing the economy on behalf of business interests.[68] Attacking liberal sympathies for the poor became the political weapon of choice.[69] Televangelists and talk show hosts began to describe a new class of "non-producers"— the media, the educational establishment, foundations, federal and state bureaucracies, and a permanent welfare constituency. These made up a liberal elite, the right charged, who were to blame for divisions in the country.[70] They portrayed the welfare state not only as the cause of moral decay, crime, and welfare dependency, but, following George Gilder, as a drain on the country's ability to generate economic growth.[71] They also por-trayed labor unions' demands for wage and benefit hikes as responsible for double digit inflation.

The war against welfare was especially useful in bidding for the white middle-income and working-class swing voters. At-tacking welfare as the *cause* of poverty, the Republicans suc-ceeded in pushing the Democratic Party rhetoric from seeking an end to poverty to discussing how to get people off welfare.[72] The new conservatism was propagated by new and refurbished foundations, legal organizations, opinion journals, newspapers, radio and television programs, and think tanks, funded by ultra-conservative corporate interests like the Coors brewing family.[73] Suddenly, groups like the Heritage Foundation, the American Enterprise Institute, the Manhattan Institute (which supported Charles Murray's *Losing Ground*), the Free Congress Foundation, the Washington Legal Foundation, and the *Washington Times* became the most widely cited experts on public policy. Journalist William Grieder later observed:

> [It] is not an exaggeration to say that democracy itself has been "captured." The forms of expression, the premises and very language of debate, not to mention the rotating cadres of experts and managers, are now owned in large measure by a relatively few interests.[74]

THE NEOCONSERVATIVE REVOLUTION

> [If] you don't have a revolution, you're going to have a country which is decaying. And I think our goal is very simple. It is our goal to replace the welfare state. Not to reform it, not to improve it, not to modify it, to replace it. To go straight at the core structure and the core values of the welfare state, and replace them with a much more powerful, much more effective system.—*Newt Gingrich, Remarks at the Young Republican Leadership Conference, March 19, 1992* [75]

The first skirmish in the war against the welfare state happened in the mid-1970s in response to a fiscal crisis in New York City. The crisis was brought on by government and banking policies that had siphoned city residents' money for out-of-state projects. It was blamed by bankers and politicians on union contracts and social services that they called inflationary. When investment bankers took over and ran the city's economy for a time, they imposed service cutbacks, reduced wages, and lowered consumption to finance private sector investment.[76] This model for New York became the model for the nation in the 1980s and 1990s.

By 1980, the neoconservative policy spinners and their religious allies had the clout to nominate Ronald Reagan and begin to dismantle the welfare state through reallocation of federal budget dollars, tax reform, deregulation, and monetary policy.[77]

Reagan wasted no time in breaking the air traffic controllers' union, PATCO, and appointing anti-labor types to the National Labor Relations Board. Under Reagan, organized labor's seat at the power-sharing table, in place since the 1930s, was officially cancelled.

Reagan's economic agenda, "supply-side economics," was a new term coined for an old Republican formula.[78] The theory was that if costs of doing business were lowered for corporations through tax and regulatory relief (including the relaxation of antitrust laws), and if people were allowed to keep more of their earnings through income tax reductions, savings would increase, resulting in a flood of new business activity that would stimulate economic growth, reduce inflation, create jobs, and balance the budget. Wealth at the top would "trickle down" in the form of more jobs at the bottom. By the time of Reagan's inauguration, this formula became what one writer called "a new economic religion" for the Republicans.[79] The Nobel Prize-winning economist James Tobin and other critics warned that supply-side policy would simply make the rich richer.[80]

Reagan's budget director David Stockman later admitted that supply-side theory was not new theory at all, but a way to "sell 'trickle down.'"[81] Stockman admitted to journalist William Grieder that "the whole thing is premised on faith ... on a belief about how the world works."[82] He also confessed that President Reagan had "only the foggiest idea of what supply-side was all about ... no one close to him had any more idea."[83] Nevertheless, Stockman implemented supply-side theory with gusto, writing a budget for the president in a record twenty-eight days. The budget proposed sweeping cuts in government programs (with the exception of the military), in regulations, and in taxes. Stockman promised his program would cut the waste and "pork" out of government.

By the time the budget emerged from congressional bargaining, the cuts fell most heavily on the poor and working class. CETA, just beginning to meet its targets, was killed at a time of almost double-digit unemployment. Programs targeted at specific constituencies for federally defined purposes were effectively broken up by converting funding into block grants to be used by state governments as they saw fit.[84] This move was the biggest blow in half a century to the mutual support arrangements set up between federal agencies, congressional committees, and advocacy groups—known in government circles as "iron triangles." However, the most powerful of these—what President Dwight D. Eisenhower called the "military-industrial complex"—was enormously enhanced during the Reagan presidency. A record $1.6 trillion was spent on defense over the next five years—the largest military buildup in peacetime history—while domestic spending was curtailed sharply.[85]

Among the cuts were not only programs for the poor but general services such as unemployment insurance, libraries, mass transit, education, recreation, and park maintenance, that most people had come to take for granted. Some welfare state programs were dismantled through regulatory changes that declared large numbers of people ineligible for entitlements. The administration's attack on disability assistance, for instance, ruled that 200,000 people—many of them severely disabled—were ineligible for the only source of income they had been receiving.[86] Budget cutters even tried to have ketchup declared a vegetable so that the cost of meeting nutritional requirements for the school lunch program could be reduced.

Reagan's 1981 Economic Recovery Tax Act was built around a reduction in the number of income-tax brackets. This was presented to the public as a "tax reduction" that would benefit the middle class. (Although the United States had the lowest tax rates of any of its economic competitors, the reduction or elimination of income taxes had long been a goal of conservatives.)[87] Stockman later admitted that the promised middle-class tax break was a Trojan horse—a ploy to divert attention from an adjustment of the top tax rate of the very rich from 70 percent (in the 1970s) down to 28 percent.[88]

The 1981 tax reform brought a massive transfer of wealth out of the lower- and middle-income groups to the very wealthy. Between 1980 and 1984, changes in tax policy had left families with incomes of less than $10,000 with a $95 loss, while families making over $200,000 had gained $17,403.[89] The reform lowered corporate taxes so much that a survey of 250 giant companies for the 1981 to 1983 period found that more than half of them escaped taxation entirely in at least one of those years, despite large profits.[90] In the 1960s, corporate income taxes were 23.4 percent of all federal revenues. Between 1983 and 1986, they fell to 8.1 percent.[91] Reduced tax revenues (estimated to have cost the federal treasury $500 billion),[92] coupled with a ballooning military budget, escalating health care costs, and deregulation of the savings and loan industry (estimated to have cost as much as $1.4 trillion)[93] sent the federal deficit through the roof. The administration was forced to borrow heavily, largely from foreign investors, to meet the continuing needs of government. It also began to borrow from the Social Security Trust Fund to meet general operating costs, which endangered the fund as it disguised the size of the deficits the Reagan administration had run up.

In spite of successive tax reforms (in 1982, 1984, 1986, 1988, 1989, 1990, and 1993) that recovered a portion of the lost tax revenue, supply-side had taken its toll. The Reagan administration's "fiscal revolution" reversed the entire postwar history of progressive debt reduction and accumulated a federal debt surpassing those of all other past administrations combined. In one decade, the United States had gone from being the world's largest creditor to being the world's largest debtor!

The Reagan administration's explicit promise to balance the federal budget by 1983 was an empty one. David Stockman's account of this period suggests that huge federal deficits were part of the supply-siders' plan to force Congress to dismantle what was left of the welfare state.[94]

By 1990, Reagan and his vice president and successor George Bush had presided over a dramatic redistribution of wealth upwards to the richest 20 percent of the population, and even more dramatically to the top 1 percent. Interest on the national debt and payments to meet the savings and loan bailout soared. The poorest 20 percent of the population saw their after-tax family incomes drop by 12 percent, while the richest 1 percent—those making on average $676,000 a year—saw their incomes go up by a staggering 136 percent (see Figure 4-1).

Supply-side's major premise was that putting more money into the hands of the wealthy and corporations would stimulate the economy and create more jobs. In fact, it had the opposite effect. With their new tax and regulatory handouts, wealthy investors built factories abroad, eliminating U.S. jobs by the thousands; they also invested in speculative real estate development, corporate mergers, and junk bonds; and they gave themselves "golden parachutes" and corporate bonuses worth billions. The immediate result was to throw the country into one of the worst recessions since the Great Depression. The unemployment rate rose to 9.7 percent in 1982, coming back down to the 5 percent range only at the end of the decade.

Meanwhile, federal subsidies for low-income housing were cut by 75 percent, creating the fiercest wave of homelessness since the Depression. Between 1980 and 1990, spending fell dramatically on welfare and unemployment, education and training, the justice system, general government, the environment, and transportation.

What did the Reagan revolution accomplish? Ninety percent of the cuts came in the first 100 days, when Reagan enjoyed unusual popularity and a compliant Congress. With the recession, Reagan's ability to cut further was limited by public

Figure 4-1

**% Changes in Average Family Incomes,
After Taxes From 1977 to 1992
(in constant dollars)**

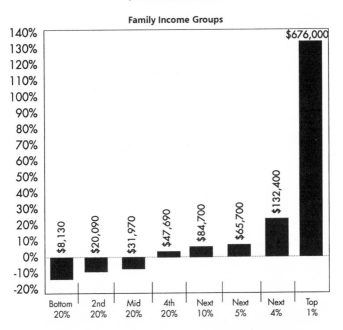

Source: Robert S. McIntyre, *Inequality and the Federal Deficit*
(Washington, D.C.: *Citizens for Tax Justice*, September 1989), p.11

opposition. Far from limiting big government, under the Reagan administration the government's growth scarcely slowed down. While programs for the poor were curtailed (with the exception of Medicaid), the military budget, Social Security, and Medicare continued to grow.

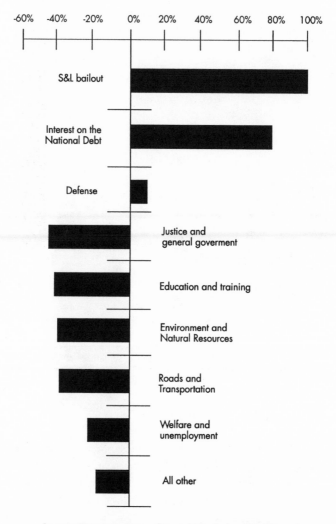

Figure 4-2
% Changes in Federal Spending, Fiscal 1980-1990
(in GNP-Adjusted Dollars, excluding Social Security OASDHI)

Source: McIntyre, *Inequality and the Federal Deficit*, p. 6

Reaganomics, however, left a time bomb inside the framework of government. The huge national debt would make any future attempts to use government spending to stimulate the economy or to relieve human suffering politically impossible. Both Republican and Democratic policy makers were lined up against using government to promote the general welfare. Promises of tax cuts replaced social services as the key to middle class support. Blaming the victims of poverty now paid political dividends.

The Reagan revolution paved the way for Republican congressional ascendancy in the 1990s. In less than thirty years the ideological center of the political establishment had moved dramatically to the right, making the question of what to do about starkly increasing inequality and deepening poverty a matter for individuals and private charities to figure out for themselves.

5

HOW POVERTY WON
THE WAR

Twelve years of Reaganomics brought new life to the financial sector but left the majority of Americans worse off than they had been in 1980. By 1992, the unwritten social pact between business, labor, and government that had stabilized the country after World War II was long gone. Faced with escalating health care costs, threats to private pension plans, declining wages, and daily reports of corporate "downsizing" (a euphemism for firing workers), a surprising 19 percent of the voters broke from the two-party system to back Ross Perot, an independent billionaire with a populist campaign against Reaganomics. Bill Clinton, a "new Democrat" who promised to rescue the beleaguered middle class from the burden of high taxes and economic insecurity, was voted in by a hair.

Clinton came not as liberalism's savior, but as its undertaker. His neoliberal program was "Reaganism lite": "streamlining" government, "ending welfare as we know it," and a health care plan written in part by the private insurance industry.

By 1993, Congress responded to rising deficits by putting permanent caps on future entitlement and discretionary spending, leaving the president empty handed in the face of a shrinking job market and the renewed threat of poverty.[1] The Republicans swept the mid-term elections in 1994, gaining both houses of Congress for the first time in forty years, eleven governorships, and fifteen state houses, despite poll results indicating widespread skepticism about GOP goals.[2]

Newt Gingrich, the new speaker of the house, opened the 104th congress announcing his intention to pass, within the first hundred days, a "Contract With America." The Contract represented the most radical restructuring of government since the New Deal—in effect, a repudiation of the idea of compassionate government. The Republican leadership took the election as a mandate for its program, even though polls indicated differently.

REAGAN REDUX

All over the Capitol these days the talk is of a Reagan revolution redux, a triumphant return by Republicans to an era of small government and more reliance than ever on the magic of the private sector. This time, of course, they say they will avoid running up $2 trillion in accumulated deficits.... Supply-side theories for raising Federal revenue by cutting taxes and stimulating the economy have risen anew. Republicans say the only problem with Ronald Reagan's vision is that no one took it far enough.

"I think Reaganomics was an incredible success," Representative Dick Armey, the Texas Republican who is now the House majority leader, told reporters over breakfast on Jan. 6. "We ought to stand up and be proud of the 80s."—*New York Times*[3]

While the New Deal had been a series of uncoordinated responses to economic crisis, the Contract With America had been several years in the making by dedicated conservatives. Most of the planks had been part of Republican language for several years. The Contract openly sought to undo everything accomplished by Roosevelt, Kennedy, Johnson, and even Nixon, in the area of public aid and social services. Gingrich's mix was both sexy—futuristic high-tech glitz—and sentimental—nineteenth century notions of private-sector services, fueled by "tough love" for those in need. Populist rhetoric was deftly put to work in the pursuit of transfering funds from the poor to the rich. A bill to slash aid to poor mothers and their children was called the "Personal Responsibility Act." A bill to redistribute wealth from the lower and middle classes to the top ten percent was called the "Job Creation and Wage Enhancement Act." A bill that would make it almost impossible to punish corporations for products that proved to be harmful to health and safety was called the "Common Sense Legal Reform Act."

The bare bones of the plan: cut government spending (with the exception of the military and corporate subsidies); transfer standard-setting and regulatory authority—especially for social programs—to the states; redistribute the tax burden downward; make market principles rather than safety and health considerations the basis for federal regulations on business; and finally, what states refuse to or cannot do leave to the private sector.

The plan to transfer authority from federal to state levels is only partial, and demonstrates how corporate freedom comes at the expense of the poor. For example, under the plan, states gain the freedom to decide their own eligibility criteria, work requirements, and even benefit levels for their welfare programs. However, they are restricted by the original plan from providing assistance to mothers under the age of eighteen, to children born after the parents had applied for welfare, to most immigrants, and to families that sought to continue collecting welfare after five years. Voting to turn the nutrition program for women, infants, and children (WIC) into a block grant, the Republicans rejected a proposal to require competitive bidding when a state buys infant formula. A major overhaul of the tort law system also federalized what had historically been a state function, making it almost impossible for non-wealthy consumers who have been harmed by some product to sue private companies for damages.

As to the national debt, the Republicans—with help from a number of Democrats—pushed a "Balanced Budget Amendment" to the Constitution, which would require the federal government to reduce the debt to zero by 2002 and to maintain balanced budgets for every year thereafter. This would require over $1 trillion in spending cuts over the next seven years, a budget so drastic it would practically eliminate every program except the military and corporate subsidies. The Balanced Budget Amendment failed to pass the Senate by only one vote after passing in the House. It succeeded in redefining the terms of budget talks from "cut fat" to "the sky's the limit."

The first victims: AFDC, Supplemental Social Insurance, mother and child nutrition programs, home energy assistance, unemployment insurance, and Medicaid. With the exception of the food stamp program (which was saved by pressure from agribusiness) and the school lunch program (now a "capped" entitlement) all of the safety net programs were to be turned into block grants at reduced amounts for the states to use as they liked.

Changes in a state's fiscal health that increase the need for safety nets, such as large plant closings, natural disasters, demographic shifts, inflation, or recessions, are no longer considered. States would be forced to choose between meeting the additional needs entirely with state funds, cutting benefits for all poor families, or denying aid to newly poor families. Faced with an estimated annual loss of nearly $100 billion by 2002 from cuts in federal aid, state and local governments would have to either raise taxes or slash education, road maintenance, libraries, recreational programs, environmental programs, park maintenance, and other basics.[4]

In general, much less is known about state legislatures than about Congress; fewer people vote in state and local elections.

State tax systems are far more regressive than the federal income tax. Without strict campaign finance reform, pork-barrel lobbying would continue at the state level. Yet the Contract casts the Republicans' strategy for "devolving power back to state and local governments" as a move toward democracy.

As state budgets were debated, fourteen states had already either cut or restricted their general assistance programs (welfare for presumably employable persons without young children), with disastrous results.[5] California voters passed a proposition denying all aid to unauthorized immigrants. The Connecticut legislature voted to shut off welfare benefits to families after twenty-one months, roll back benefits to levels of the late 1980s, and require all welfare recipients to be fingerprinted.[6] The state's highest court upheld a 1992 law that allowed cities and towns to cut off welfare benefits to able-bodied individuals after nine months, stating that Connecticut had no constitutional responsibility to care for its poorest citizens.[7] Facing the most drastic budget cuts in half a century, New York's future was compared to the "shock treatment" that devastated postcommunist Eastern European economies.[8]

Who would pick up the pieces of the human wreckage left from government downsizing? The Republicans' answer: either private companies, private charity, or volunteers. Yet most private charities were already stretched to the bone and heavily dependent on government funding (which would be cut). Gift giving to human service organizations dropped considerably between 1994 and 1995, and voluntarism had succumbed to longer working hours and sheer survival.[9] Meanwhile, proposed reductions in government record keeping and information gathering would sabotage the ability of advocacy groups to monitor economic, social, environmental, and physical health.[10] Back on the private side, corporations recorded a measly 4.7 percent of all charitable giving.[11]

Gingrich had pledged that Republicans would balance the budget *and* provide $189 billion in tax relief over five years.[12] While a $500 per year per child tax credit was offered for the "middle class," about half the Contract's tax cuts would go to the top 10 percent of U.S. families, and nearly one third to the top 2 percent.[13] Some Republicans, however, were pushing to go even farther. "Our challenge," said Rep. Bill Archer, chair of the House Ways and Means Committee, "is to do no less than pull the current income tax code out by its roots and throw it away so it can never grow back."[14]

THE PERSONAL RESPONSIBILITY ACT

Some of the most radical neocon thinking went into the Personal Responsibility Act, the House Republican bill that sought to reform the major safety net programs. Charles Murray was invited to speak to the House Republicans early in their deliberations. Among the act's provisions were the following:

• Elimination of AFDC's entitlement status, which meant that no child or family, regardless of the depth of the family's poverty or the parent's willingness to work, would be assured of receiving assistance if a state ran out of money.

• Capping AFDC spending at 1994 levels for the next five years and repealing the mandate for states to match federal funds.

• Prohibiting mothers under eighteen from receiving grants for children born out of wedlock, as well as children born to families already receiving AFDC or who had received aid at any time during the ten-month period before the birth of the child. If a husband were to desert his pregnant wife, thereby forcing her to apply for cash assistance, she would be prohibited from receiving any aid for the newborn—even though the child was conceived before the parents starting receiving assistance.

• A five-year limit on the time a family could receive welfare, regardless of whether the parents have been able to find work.

• Eliminating cash assistance through the SSI program for 80 percent of disabled children who would otherwise become eligible in future years, and for people whose disabilities stem from alcoholism or drug abuse.

• Replacing federal child welfare programs with block grants, thus ending the assurance of foster care payments for children from AFDC-eligible families who cannot safely live at home, as well as payments to families that adopt children with special needs.

• Denying most forms of assistance to most immigrants and to all immigrants without papers.

• Repealing the Job Opportunities and Basic Skills (JOBS) program, which had required states to provide a range of education, training, and work programs for AFDC parents. No new resources would be committed to expanding welfare-to-work programs.

• Reducing federal resources for child care, a critical component of any initiative to move welfare recipients into the workforce.

Given the fact that between 1970 and 1995, AFDC benefits in the median state fell 47 percent. After adjusting for inflation, these cuts would mean severe hardship for millions more and put in real doubt the survival of those already in poverty.

In the spring and summer of 1995, as the public began to learn what these cuts would mean, protests broke out in cities across the country. They were often large, but poorly coordinated and ignored by the press. Liberal research groups and foundations sought to sound the alarm in Congress and state legislatures. But in politics and public relations, it's money that matters. In contrast with the Vietnam War era, the major media "manufactured consent,"[15] ignoring dissident voices and replacing news analysis with shallow, one-sided chatter. The two-party system, if not representative democracy itself, was beginning to look like an endless infomercial for the conservative attack.[16]

THE NEW WORLD DISORDER?

As noted earlier, capitalism naturally results in inequality. Chronic poverty for some, as well as periodic recessions and depressions which have thrown more people into poverty, has been continuous throughout the system's history. Only twice in this century have there been major attempts in the United States to reduce poverty, and these occurred only when people organized to force their elected representatives to curb some of capital's power. Mass protest that disrupted business-as-usual and ballot box reform have both been necessary.

The government has several ways of curbing corporate power. It has put direct controls on capital's prerogatives through such measures as price controls (as in World War II), antitrust legislation, and prohibition of antilabor practices like hiring scabs or starting company unions. Another approach is through use of indirect controls, such as standards for the conduct of business and penalties for failure to meet such standards (often included in labor, environmental, and consumer legislation). Washington has also set up programs, like the NLRB and the CAPs, to bolster or protect trade unions and community groups.

It remains to be explained why these curbs on capital are not working now. Why have groups concerned with labor, poor people, consumers, and the environment been unable to stop the wholesale destruction of programs that, if not perfect, were at least moving in the direction of reducing inequality?

The new U.S. social policy arrives amid changes that have been occurring in the global capitalist economy since 1970. Call it globalization, postindustrialism, or the new world order; it is a major restructuring of the capitalist system, the most extensive since the industrial revolution of the nineteenth century.[17]

The quarter century following World War II was a period of unusual stability and growth in production and consumption—nearly 5 percent a year—and low unemployment, with rising wages and benefits.[18] The key to this postwar system was the dominant role played by the United States in the world economy. Having been spared invasion, the United States could afford to supply capital, goods, and technology to rebuild Europe and Japan. In turn, it reaped the rewards of new markets for its goods and services. The U.S. military contained the spread of unfriendly influences—especially communism—as the devastated industrial economies in Europe and Japan were rebuilt. Meanwhile, the U.S. dollar served as the measure of international currency convertibility, keeping the system of aid and trade steady.

All this came to an end by the beginning of the 1970s. Japan and Germany challenged U.S. dominance and Nixon was forced to end the Bretton-Woods Agreement, under which the dollar had served as the measure of international convertibility. Following the OPEC oil cartel's decision to raise world oil prices in 1973, the capitalist system entered a troubled period of slower growth rates, spiraling inflation, and volatile currency markets.

Corporations looked for different ways of recovering their profits. They replaced workers with machines and moved to cheap labor zones abroad—where they could also escape labor and environmental regulations and enjoy lucrative tax breaks. More profits were found in merging with other companies and then downsizing, and in engaging in new and risky forms of financial speculation. According to several critics, the piling up of speculative profits (90 percent of all international transactions) has come to dominate contemporary capitalism. All sense of "a larger public responsibility" has been dropped, as the very productive capacity of nations has been strapped.[19]

Corporate restructuring has been boosted by technological advances in telecommunications, computerization, and transportation. These have made it possible to transfer money, people, products, and even offices and factories anywhere in the world at breakneck speed, and to increase productivity while shedding workers. This acceleration of global competition has led to new production and marketing techniques, called "just-in-time inventories," in which companies compete by turning out smaller batches of products for specialized markets with quicker turnaround times.

The result is a new form of capitalist structure with a new international division of labor that forces U.S. workers to compete with low-wage workers around the world. This development appears at a "new stage of global finance ... one with the 'freest-flowing and most sophisticated (that is, complicated) financial markets the world has ever known.'"[20] Three global trading and currency blocs have also appeared, made up of clusters of nations: the European Economic Community, Japan and Southeast Asia, and the Western hemisphere. Each bloc has its own "first" and "third" worlds, composed of highly developed industrialized or "core" countries and poorer or less developed "periphery" countries that are exploited for their cheap labor and resources. Each bloc tends to be dominated by one of the countries in the cluster—Germany in Europe, Japan in Asia, and the United States in the Western hemisphere.

This "new world order" has resulted in rising rates of structural (permanent as opposed to cyclical) unemployment and underemployment. It has also led to declining wages for the majority of low-skilled workers across the world. Even highly skilled and educated workers have fallen into the pit in some countries.[21]

The worst crisis of unemployment, underemployment, and wage decline has been in the third world, where the already severe gap between rich and poor, both within those countries, and between them and the industrialized ones, has widened into a Grand Canyon. According to the United Nations, the total number of people living in poverty is estimated at one-fifth of the total world population, with 90 percent of them in Asia and Africa.[22]

In the United States and Britain, increasing poverty has come despite some economic growth. This delinking of national growth and national well-being is unprecedented.[23] With the exception of Britain, most of the Western European nations—still under pressure from trade unions and working-class-oriented parties—have maintained their safety nets, high wages, and environmental and labor regulations, but have suffered unusually high double-digit unemployment rates.[24] The United States and Britain (whose ruling elites mimic each other) have maintained single-digit rates of unemployment (though still higher than in earlier decades) but at the expense of increasing levels of absolute and relative poverty, as well as greater insecurity for working people.[25]

Rising inequality within and between nations has led, in turn, to higher death and crime rates, soaring numbers of "economic refugees" moving within and between countries, dire ethnic tensions, and war.

Another result of the globalization process is the unprecedented power enjoyed by transnational corporations today. The largest control assets and take in revenues that dwarf the gross domestic products of entire nations.

THE NEW IMPERIALISTS

Global corporations are the first secular institutions run by men (and a handful of women) who think and plan on a global scale.... A relatively few companies with worldwide connections dominate the four intersecting webs of global commercial activity on which the new world economy largely rests: the Global Cultural Bazaar; the Global Shopping Mall; the Global Workplace; and the Global Financial Network.... These worldwide webs of economic activity have already achieved a degree of global integration never before achieved by any world empire or nation-state. The driving force behind each of them can be traced in large measure to the same few hundred corporate giants with headquarters in the United States, Japan, Germany, France, Switzerland, the Netherlands, and the United Kingdom. The combined assets of the top 300 firms now make up roughly a quarter of the productive assets in the world.—*Richard J. Barnet and John Cavanagh* [26]

This kind of power is, in effect, a new kind of world government in the making—unaccountable to any public. In a series of transnational forums called *regimes*, corporate elites meet to transact world business. These regimes are deforming democratic institutions across the world, making it harder for governments to protect the interests of workers, consumers, and the poor, and eroding even the process of representation. For example, consumer advocate Ralph Nader has pointed out that one of these regimes, the newly created World Trade Organization (WTO), is a three-person tribunal that sits in secret judgement on world trade disputes in Geneva, Switzerland. Accountable to no elected body, it can nullify labor and environmental regulations that nations or even lower units of government attempt to impose on companies that do business within their borders whenever such regulations are successfully challenged by another nation as "barriers to free trade." According to Colorado Senator Hank Brown, the only member of Congress to accept Nader's challenge to read and answer questions about the 550-page treaty that set up the WTO, "this treaty [the Uruguay Round of the General Agreement on Tariffs and Trade] creates a new world government without fair representation for the United States and an international court system without due process."[27]

For third world nations this is nothing new; international financial institutions have long called the shots, resulting in the devastation of whole economies. Now, however, even the economies of industrialized nations are subject to the whims of global financial speculators and the domestic agendas of foreign governments—including the United States, the new number-one debtor nation. "To a degree rarely seen before," observed *New York Times* journalist David Sanger, "bond traders and the currency markets are driving policy, rather than reacting to it."[28] The International Labor Organization has explained how speculative investment affects national monetary policies:

> A significant fraction of investors now have a real alternative to investing their money either long-term or short-term. When both short-term and long-term [interest] rates seem unattractively low, flows of funds into these more speculative types of investment are likely to increase dramatically. As a consequence, long-term investors as a group are now able to extract an inflation premium that was not available before the explosive growth of these speculative markets, and this has created a permanent tendency towards high long-term interest rates across the entire world economy, rates which lead directly to higher rates of unemployment and slower rates of global growth.[29]

For example, take the Federal Reserve's decisions to raise interest rates seven times in 1994-1995, and the pressure to pass a Balanced Budget Amendment. Federal Reserve chairman Alan Greenspan openly acknowledged the pressure from international currency markets in speech to the Economic Club of New York in June 1995. It would be a mistake, he told them, to stimulate business activity by lowering interest rates if that led investors to pull money out of the United States, weakening an already shaky dollar.[30]

Similarly, the idea of a balanced budget amendment was opposed by eleven past and present presidents of the American Economics Association, seven Nobel Prize winners, and hundreds of other top economists.[31] Still, the heads of foreign banks and governments have been pressuring for measures to reduce the deficit quickly, even at the expense of slowing down the economy and increasing poverty and unemployment.[32]

FIRST AMONG EQUALS, OR LAST AMONG UNEQUALS?

It is hard to know whether this is a good news story or a bad news story, but here it is: The Agency for International Development, which spent the cold war fighting Communism with foreign aid and helping poor countries like Bangladesh immunize children, has found a new customer for its services: America's inner cities.... The good news is that A.I.D. has something to offer. The bad news is that parts of Los Angeles, Boston and Baltimore now need it as much as Bangladesh.—*New York Times*[33]

Until now, the postwar welfare states of Europe have made the United States look sick in comparison. But as Europeans protest unheard-of unemployment rates, more of their governments are beginning to look enviously to this country as a model for employment growth, more or less accepting the poverty, inequality, and deteriorating working conditions that accompany it.[34] Since these governments are increasingly pressured by international currency markets to reduce spending, they will have to cut welfare benefits to increase employment—not just aid to subsistence-level families but universal health care, generous family leaves for child rearing, and paid six-week vacations, which their populations now take for granted.[35]

Big business and government have always been intertwined, but in recent years this relationship has become much more intense and open. Government officials increasingly accept political guidance directly from corporate figures—indeed, appoint them to high offices or let them ghostwrite legislation. On the Democratic side:

• Treasury Secretary Robert Rubin, former co-chair of the Wall Street investment firm of Goldman Sachs (approximate wealth—$50-$100 million), serves as President Clinton's chief economic advisor.

• Ron Brown, former Chairman of the Democratic Party and a partner in one of Washington's most powerful corporate law firms, was appointed commerce secretary. Before this, he represented both Japanese manufacturers and the Haitian Duvalier dictatorship.

• Mickey Kantor, U.S. Trade Representative, had previously represented corporations before state and local regulators for his law firm, a registered lobbyist for the Tokyo-based NEC Corporation, among others.[36]

Just a sampling of Republican corporate and financial ties:

• Newt Gingrich rose to power with the support of the multinational Southwire Company, the nation's largest supplier of copper wire and cable and a notorious violator of federal environmental regulations. Southwire would directly benefit from deregulation measures promised in the Contract.[37]

• Contributors to a tax-exempt "research" foundation, Better America, set up by Senate majority leader and presidential candidate Robert Dole, include a virtual who's who of corporate America. Among the $100,000 donors were chairs or CEOs of such corporations as AT&T, BankAmerica, RJR Nabisco, Schering-Plough, Philip Morris, and USX Corporation.[38]

• During the drafting of legislation that effectively deregulated industry in the spring of 1995, Republican legislators (despite House rules to the contrary) permitted lawyers for all of the top firms to take an active role in committee functions.[39]

FIELD DAY FOR CORPORATE LOBBYISTS

Washington's corporate and business lobbyists represent a myriad of often clashing interests. But there is striking unanimity about the first 100 days of the new Congress: things, they say, could hardly have gone better. As members of a coalition called the Thursday Group, lobbyists worked hand in glove with the House Republican leadership to build grass-roots support for the Contract With America, earning chits they hope will prove useful in the months ahead.... The House passed measures that had been on the lobbyists' wish lists for years, lowering business taxes, reining in Government regulators and limiting the scope of civil law suits that cost companies billions of dollars each year.—*New York Times*[40]

CHANGING COURSE

These are dangerous times. To quote Walter Russell Mead:

If political leaders cannot control their economies to assure rising living standards they must and will play the nationalist card in the contest for power. This is obviously true today in the case of countries like Russia and Serbia. But it could well be true tomorrow in places like Germany, France, and the United States if the inherent instability of an international economy dominated by unregulated private capital flows should plunge the world into a series of major economic crises.[41]

Politics may be defined as the process through which people make decisions about the allocation of scarce resources: "who gets what, when, and how," as political scientist Harold Lasswell has explained. Reducing poverty and inequality means redefining the bases of national and world economies from profit for the few, to serving the aspirations of the majority of the world's people for healthy, secure, and fulfilling lives, and preserving the earth for future generations. To realize this new vision, millions of people, in all countries, will have to take part in restructuring the current relations of power—between governments and the governed, between employers and employees, and across both color and gender lines. Compared to this task, the Republican reforms are just a game of musical chairs where the poorest always lose. After each round, a new layer of the population finds itself counted out.

It is only fairly recently that national and international researchers have been documenting the costs and tracing them to unequal distribution of power and wealth.[42] Those interested in alternative to pro-business think tanks can refer to a growing list of research institutes that offer in-depth analyses of public policy issues and policy prescriptions.[43] Seminars are offered by trade unions and religious organizations, as well as by independent organizations set up for the purpose of teaching economics; one of the best is the Massachusetts-based Center for Popular Economics. Information and discussion on the economy are also available on a number of Internet forums, including PeaceNet, EcoNet, LaborNet, and HandsNet.

For those who are ready to get active, some national and international coalitions and networks of local organizations have begun to grow with the goal of pushing for full employment and a restructured economy. The National Jobs for All Coalition seeks to bring together all of the single-issue organizations with a stake in full employment. The Federation for Industrial Retention and Renewal, formed out of numerous local efforts across the country to save plants from closing, organizes local community plans for restoring industry. The Industrial Areas Foundation (IAF) and Association of Community Organizations for Reform Now (ACORN) have built local organizations in dozens of states that challenge entrenched political leadership and engage in community rebuilding efforts. World Hunger Year seeks to influence policy makers by sharing innovative solutions to hunger and poverty, developed by grassroots organizations across the country.

Labor Secretary Robert Reich has estimated that U.S. corporate subsidies cost the Treasury more than $100 billion a year—more than double the cost of the federal welfare and food stamp programs combined. To challenge the powerful transnational corporations would take international cooperation far beyond anything tried by the United Nations. Yet resistance is starting to take shape.

Through nongovernmental organizations (NGOs), people around the world are straining to enforce legal and ethical standards of government accountability on corporations, which are publicly chartered and have received enormous public subsidies. Some organizations have developed programmatic demands that focus on the corporate structure itself, such as putting representatives of workers, communities, and environmental advocates on corporate boards. For runaway industries, the National Jobs for All Coalition has advocated a "stay or pay" policy that requires companies to negotiate with the workers and communities in areas that they plan to leave, and to compensate them for the losses that will be incurred.

Accounting is another area that cries out for reform: public pressure can force the inclusion of the social and environmental costs that are now "externalized" into corporate accounting systems as part of the costs of doing business. Guidelines for doing this have been published by the United Nations.

Restoring the U.S. corporate income tax to the levels that prevailed in the 1950s would reduce nearly two-thirds of the current deficit and free up that money to meet human needs and create jobs. International financial transactions based on speculation is a growing practice that threatens to capsize the already-shaky world economy; taxing only one-tenth of one penny on the dollar of foreign exchange transactions would raise $1 billion each trading day—nearly $250 billion per year—an amount that could finance the UN, and all of its development and relief programs, while contributing to deficit reduction around the world.[44]

Other proposals focus on the income gap. A bill introduced in the British parliament would limit corporate executives from exceeding twenty times the average pay of their nonmanagerial employees. In the United States, the Share the Wealth Project is promoting the idea that all incomes for tax purposes should be pegged to the minimum wage. Maximum income could then be capped at a reasonable level and the excess recovered through the income tax system; this would give taxpayers an incentive to raise the minimum wage to a liveable level.[45] Others have proposed direct taxes on wealth similar to what eleven other industrialized countries now have.[46]

The most wasteful and destructive generator of poverty is military spending. All the horror stories about weakened national security cannot conceal the fact that if all U.S. military spending ended today, Washington would still have the world's most lethal arsenal and enough nuclear weapons to kill everyone in the world several times over. Military spending produces fewer jobs than spending in the civilian sector, while it drains the Treasury of the resources needed to stimulate growth and meet human needs.

The United States is the world's largest supplier of weapons. Reducing our own arsenal would help to reduce world poverty, since military spending now eats up a greater and greater proportion of the treasuries of those countries that can least afford it.

For decades, peace groups like the National Commission for Economic Conversion and Disarmament have offered proposals for drastically reducing the military without weakening the national defense and without leaving defense industry workers shut out.

New forms of opposition spring up every day. Some groups work at the purely local level, developing "communities of

resistance" around issues like toxic waste dumping, plant closings, social service cutbacks, and the destruction of indigenous
communities and cultures by agribusiness and big oil. Others
seek to resist the end-of-the-century plagues of drug trafficking,
street crime, and health problems spread by poverty and unemployment—from AIDS to tuberculosis. Many of these groups
have since developed alternatives to the destructive practices
they set out to resist. World Hunger Year, a national antipoverty
advocacy group, has collected case histories of many of these
local community-building efforts across the country.

In many places, local resistance movements have broadened
to build sustainable communities to meet people's needs while
providing socially useful work and a healthy environment. For
example, local organizations that had come together around
plant closings have formed the national Federation for Industrial
Retention and Renewal, a network of organizations located in
every region of the United States. The Federation provides technical help and supports networking among local groups, sharing
strategies for grassroots community economic development.

Among other things, they have had to learn how to research
where their community's tax dollars are going. Several of these
groups learned that large firms used community development
block grants to help them move out of the area, costing many
local workers their jobs. They took this information to Congress
to change the law so that such block grants can't be used to
remove local jobs.[47]

THE LOW ROAD AND THE HIGH ROAD

Time and again, major newspapers have run articles on Cleveland
the "comeback city." While paying attention to new skyscrapers, convention centers, and entertainment districts, they have overlooked a
more important story. Over the last 15 years Cuyahoga County has

lost 40% of its manufacturing jobs; and the county's poverty rate has increased by 49%.... Unable to work under old rules in a new global economy, economic development offices are desperately grasping at straws. Those straws have been deregulation, lowered standards, and tax giveaways designed to attract investment—any kind of investment.

It's what we've called the "low road" strategy of competing with third world labor markets by creating third world conditions in our cities. The price is enormous.... Our cities contain huge pools of potentially productive resources. They have accumulated the fruits of generations of private and public investment that have created business sectors with skilled workers, plant and equipment, and related infrastructures. They have grown public and private institutions designed to service the needs of these businesses, their employees and the communities that surround them.... All of this ... is a foundation for building a pro- gressive economic development strategy. We've called this the "high road"—mobilizing all these resources through a democratic industrial policy designed to shape a high wage, high skill future. —*Jim Benn, Federation for Industrial Retention and Renewal*[48]

Many in the labor movement now see organizing globally as a way to prevent companies from playing one country's work- force against another. Ideally, workers in different countries employed by the same multinational company could organize internationally to support each others' demands for better wages and working conditions. Meetings between groups of U.S. work- ers with their counterparts in Mexico, El Salvador, Guatemala, the Dominican Republic, and Haiti are moving in that direction.

In recent years, United Nations conferences on development- related issues (such as 1995's World Summit on Social Develop- ment and the Conference on the Decade of Women) have seen increased activity by grassroots NGOs. Taking the issues of the poor into the deliberations of official (government-sponsored) conferences, NGOs have developed vast networking appara- tuses through alternative summits and by means of the Internet. A global organization of indigenous peoples whose traditional cultures and economies face extinction due to Western development schemes is one result.

These are only small indications of what is possible when people uncover the true causes of poverty and work together toward positive solutions. The system may appear unbeatable, but it has a thousand weak points. When concerned people organize and share information, they become a challenge to poverty and inequality. Every challenge carries the seeds of a solution.

In the government campaigns of past decades, the terms were dictated by official experts. That *cold war* on poverty is over. For the growing poor population, the real fight is just beginning.

NOTES

CHAPTER 1: CLASS AND POVERTY: MYTHS AND REALITIES

1. George Bush, quoted in Benjamin DeMott, "The Myth of Classlessness," *New York Times*, 10 November 1990, p. A23.
2. Charles W. Dunn and Martin W. Slann, *American Government: A Comparative Approach* (New York: HarperCollins College Publishers, 1994), p. 47.
3. Benjamin DeMott, "The Myth of Classlessness."
4. Russell Baker, "The Middle Riddle," *New York Times*, 18 January 1992, p. A23.
5. The latest collection of this data is found in U.S. Bureau of Census, *Current Population Reports*, Series P60-184, *Money Income of Households, Families and Persons in the United States: 1992* (Washington D.C.: U.S. Government Printing Office, 1993).
6. The Census Bureau defines a household as consisting of all persons who occupy a housing unit whether related or unrelated. The occupants live and eat together and enter the unit through a separate entrance.
7. Although the Census Bureau carefully constructs its population sample so as to be scientifically representative of the total population of the United States, it can never be totally accurate and suffers from several distortions. Estimates from a sample may differ from figures from a complete census using the same questionnaires, instructions and enumerators. Nonsampling

errors may result from inability to obtain information about all cases in the sample; vague definitions; differences in the interpretation of questions; confusion, poor memory, or sabotage by respondents; errors made in data collection such as in recording or coding the data; errors made in processing data; errors made in estimating values for missing data; and failure to represent all units with the sample. See U.S. Bureau of the Census, *Current Population Reports*, Series P60-184, *Money Income of Households, Families, and Persons in the United States: 1992* (Washington, D.C.: U.S. Government Printing Office, 1993), pp. D-2-D-3.

8. U.S. Bureau of the Census, *Current Population Reports*, Series P60-188, *Income, Poverty and Valuation of Noncash Benefits: 1993*, p. xii.

9. Frederick R. Strobel, *Upward Dreams, Downward Mobility: The Economic Decline of the American Middle Class* (Lanham, MD: Rowman & Littlefield Publishers, Inc., 1993), pp. 42-43.

10. Ibid., p. 43.

11. William O'Hare, Taynia Mann, Kathryn Porter, Robert Greenstein, *Real Life Poverty in America: Where the American Public Would Set the Poverty Line* (Washington, D.C.: Center on Budget and Policy Priorities, 1990.)

12. Jon Nordheimer, "From Middle Class to Jobless: A Sense of Pride is Shattered," *New York Times*, 13 April 1992, p. A1.

13. Steve Lohr, "Recession Puts a Harsh Spotlight on Hefty Pay of Top Executives," *New York Times*, 20 January 1992, p. 1.

14. John R. Oravec, "Executive Pay Up 26% Tops Workers 104 Times," *AFL-CIO News*, 25 May 1992, p. 10.

15. U.S. Bureau of the Census, *Current Population Reports*, Series P60-188, *Income, Poverty, and Valuation of Noncash Benefits: 1993* (Washington, D.C.: U.S. Government Printing Office, 1994), Table 5.

16. U.S. Bureau of the Census, *Current Population Reports*, Series P60-184, *Money Income of Households, Families and Persons in the United States: 1992* (Washington, D.C.: U.S. Government Printing Office, 1993), Table 29.

17. Felicity Barringer, "A Census Disparity for Asians in U.S.," *New York Times*, 20 September 1992, p. 36. The author of the Census report attributed the lower earnings of Asian-Americans to the fact that they are underrepresented in the skilled crafts and in the executive suites.

18. Lars Osberg, *Economic Inequality in the United States* (Armonk, NY: M.E. Sharpe, 1984), pp. 38-49.

19. Lawrence Mishel and Jared Bernstein, *The State of Working America, 1992-93* (Washington, D.C.: Economic Policy Institute; Armonk, NY: M.E. Sharpe, 1993), Table 5.3, p. 256.

20. Sylvia Nasar, "Fed Gives New Evidence of 80's Gains by Richest," *New York Times*, 21 April 1992, p. 1. The Federal Reserve survey from which this data was taken was conducted on a sample of 3,143 households, concentrating especially on families with very high incomes who are typically undercounted in most surveys. The top 1 percent of households—834,000—was worth about $5.7 trilion, while the bottom 90 percent—84 million households—was worth $4.8 trillion. However, because of the difficulty in getting accurate data on wealth and potential sampling error, researchers

issued several caveats about accepting the validity of the data. See also Mishel and Bernstein, *The State of Working America, 1992-93*, p. 255.

21. Mishel and Bernstein, p. 255.

22. U.S. Bureau of the Census, *Current Population Reports*, Series P-70, No. 22 (Washington, D.C.: U.S. Government Printing Office, 1990), cited in Lenneal J. Henderson, "African Americans in the Urban Milieu: Conditions, Trends and Development Needs," Billy J. Tidwell, ed., *The State of Black America, 1994* (Washington, D.C.: The National Urban League, 1994), p. 20.

23. Robert Pear, "Rich Got Richer in 80's; Others Held Even," *New York Times*, 11 January 1991, p. 1.

24. U.S. Bureau of the Census, *Current Population Reports*, Series P60-184, *Money Income of Households, Families, and Persons in the United States: 1992*, Table 22.

25. Figures taken from U.S. Department of Commerce, Bureau of the Census, *Minority-Owned Business Enterprises—Black* MB 87-1 (Washington, D.C.: U.S. Government Printing Office, 1990). Cited in Lenneal J. Henderson, "Empowerment Thourgh Enterprise: African-American Business Development" in *The State of Black America, 1993* (Washington, D.C.: National Urban League, 1993), p. 94.

26. William D. Bradford, "Dollars for Deeds: Prospects and Prescriptions for African-American Financial Institutions" in *The State of Black America, 1994*, p. 31.

27. A.H. Jones, *Wealth of a Nation To Be: The American Colonies on the Eve of Revolution* (New York: Columbia University Press, 1980), p. 317.

28. Jason DeParle, "Sharp Increase Along the Border of Poverty," *New York Times*, 31 March 1994, p. A18.

29. Christopher Jencks, a sociologist who has studied poverty, has conjectured that on the basis of such data, more people may be becoming so discouraged that they are dropping out of the labor market. See Louis Uchitelle, "Unequal Pay Widesprad in the U.S.," *New York Times*, 14 August 1990, p. D1.

30. Donald Barlett and James Steele, "Rules Shaping the Economy Stacked Against Middle Class," *Charlotte Observer*, 24 November 1991, p. 1A.

31. U.S. Bureau of the Census, *Current Population Reports*, Series P-60, No. 177, *Trends in Relative Income: 1964-1989* (Washington, D.C.: U.S. Government Printing Office, 1991), p. 3. Cited in Frederick R. Strobel, *Upward Dreams, Downward Mobility*, p. 47.

32. Sylvia Nasar, "The 1980's: A Very Good Time for the Very Rich," *New York Times*, 5 March 1992, p. 1.

33. Robert Pear, "Rich Got Richer in 80's; Others Held Even," *New York Times*, 11 January 1991, p. 1.

34. Paul R. Krugman, economist at the Massachusetts Institute of Technology, quoted in Sylvia Nasar, "Fed Gives New Evidence of 80's Gains by Richest," *New York Times*, 21 April 1992, p. 1.

35. Brett D. Fromson, "Where Wall Street Goes to Play," *Washington Post National Weekly Edition*, 22-28 August 1994, p. 22.

36. Sylvia Nasar, "Those Born Wealthy or Poor Usually Stay So, Studies Say," *New York Times*, 18 May 1992, p. 1.

37. John Bound and Richard B. Freeman, "What Went Wrong? The Erosion of Relative Earnings and employment Among Young Black Men in the 1980s,"

Quarterly Journal of Economics, 1992, cited in Marc Breslow, "The Racial Divide Widens: Why African Americans Have Lost Ground," *Dollars and Sense*, No. 197 (January/February, 1995), p. 11.

38. Davide H. Swinton, "The Economic Status of African Americans During the Reagan-Bush Era: Withered Opportunities, Limited Outcomes, and Uncertain Outlook," *The State of Black America, 1993*, p. 135.

39. U.S. Bureau of the Census, *Current Population Reports*, Series P60-184, *Money Income of households, families, and Persons in the United States: 1992*, Table 22.

40. U.S. Bureau of the Census, *Current Population Reports*, Series P-60-185, *Poverty in the United States: 1992* (Washington, D.C.: U.S. Government Printing Office, 1993), Table 3.

41. Michael D. Yates, *Longer Hours, Fewer Jobs: Employment and Unemployment in the United States* (New York: Monthly Review Press, 1994), p. 84.

42. Bernard Sanders, "Whither American Democracy," Congressional reprint. First published in the *Los Angeles Times*, 16 January 1994.

43. James Madison, *Notes of Debates in the Federal Convention of 1787* (Athens, OH: Ohio University Press, 1976), p. 194.

44. Lee Atwater, "The South In 1984," an unpublished analysis of Southern politics prepared for the Reagan-Bush campaign, cited in Thomas Byrne Edsall with Mary D. Edsall, *Chain Reaction: The Impact of Race, Rights, and Taxes on American Politics* (New York: W.W. Norton & Co., 1992), p. 221.

45. Lillian Breslow Rubin has described the effects on working class families of such internalized self-doubt and alienation in *Worlds of Pain: Life in the Working Class Family* (New York: Basic Books, 1977). Dr. Harvey Brenner of Johns Hopkins University has, over the last twenty years, documented rises in the unemployment level (economic failure experienced as individual failure) with increased rates of heart attacks, alcoholism, and other stress-related diseases. See M. Harvey Brenner, "Economy, Society and Health," paper prepared for the Conference on Society and Health, Harvard School of Public Health, 16 October 1992.

46. Sheila Collins, *The Rainbow Challenge: The Jackson Campaign and the Future of U.S. Politics* (New York: Monthly Review Press, 1987); see especially Chapter 8, pp. 228-253.

CHAPTER 2: DECIDING WHO'S POOR

1. Michael Harrington, *The Other America* (New York: Macmillan, 1962).

2. John C. Donovan, *The Politics of Poverty* (New York: Pegasus, 1967), p. 96.

3. From *Autobiography of Black Hawk as dictated by himself to Antoine LeClair*, J.B. Patterson, ed., excerpted in T.C. McLuhan, *Touch the Earth: A Self Portrait of Indian Existence* (New York: Pocket Books, 1972).

4. Majid Rehnema, "Poverty," in *The Development Dictionary*, Wolfgang Sachs, ed. (London: Zed Books, 1992), p. 160.

5. Department of Economic and Social Development, United Nations, *Report on the World Social Situation 1993* (New York: United Nations), p. 28.

6. Sharon M. Oster, Elizabeth E. Lake, and Conchita Gene Oksman, *The*

Definition and Measurement of Poverty, Vol. 1: A Review (Boulder, CO: Westview Press, 1978), p. 5.

7. A typical worker employed in the manufacturing sector in El Salvador earned forty cents an hour in 1992. This wage provided for only 15 percent of a family's basic survival needs. In Haiti, an even poorer country, the typical wage is fourteen cents an hour. Wages like these are often paid by U.S.-owned companies who have transfered their labor-intensive operations to these poorer countries with the help of the U.S. government. For a study of how this is done, see the reports *Paying to Lose Our Jobs* (September 1992) and *Free Trade's Hidden Secrets: Why We Are Losing Our Shirts* (November 1993), available from the National Labor Committee, 15 Union Square West, New York, NY 10003.

8. George M. Frederickson, *White Supremacy: A Comparative Study in American and South African History* (Oxford: Oxford University Press, 1981), pp. 7, 9-10.

9. Michael B. Katz, *The Undeserving Poor: From the War on Poverty to the War on Welfare* (New York: Basic Books/HarperCollins, 1986), p. 116.

10. Richard May, *1993 Poverty and Income Trends* (Washington, D.C.: Center on Budget and Policy Priorities, March 1995), p. 11.

11. Most of the data in this chapter is taken from U.S. Bureau of the Census, *Current Population Reports,* Series P60-188, *Income, Poverty, and Valuation of Noncash Benefits: 1993* (Washington, D.C.: U.S. Government Printing Office, 1995).

12. Ibid., Figure 2, p. xv.

13. Ibid., p. xvii.

14. Ibid., Table 8. The category "Hispanic origin" is the Census Bureau's wording and not the author's.

15. Timothy M. Smeeding and Lee Rainwater, "Cross-national Trends in Income, Poverty and Dependency: The Evidence for Young Adults in the Eighties," *The Luxembourg Income Study,* Working Paper #67. Prepared for the Joint Center for Policy Studies Conference on Poverty and Social Marginality, Washington, D.C., September 20-21, 1991. See also Center on Social Welfare Policy and Law, "Childhood Poverty and Public Transfers in International Perspective," May 1991.

16. U.S. Bureau of the Census, *Current Population Reports,* Series P60-188, 1993, Table 8.

17. Isabel Wilkerson, "First Born, Fast Grown: The Manful Life of Nicholas, 10," *New York Times,* 4 April 1993, p. 1.

18. U.S. Bureau of the Census, *Current Population Reports,* Series P60-188, 1993, p. xv.

19. Peter Applebome, "Deep South and Down Home, But It's a Ghetto All the Same," *New York Times,* 21 August 1993, p. 1.

20. U.S. Bureau of the Census, *Current Population Reports,* Series P60-188, 1993, pp. xv, xvii.

21. Isabel Wilkerson, "As Farms Falter, Rural Homelessness Grows," *New York Times,* 2 April 1989, p. 1.

22. Richard May, *1993 Poverty and Income Trends,* p. 77.

23. Jason DeParle, "Sharp Increase Along the Borders of Poverty," *New York Times,* 31 March 1994, p. A18.

24. John E. Schwarz and Thomas J. Volgy, *The Forgotten Americans: Thirty Million Working Poor in the Land of Opportunity* (New York: W.W. Norton, 1992), p. 3.

25. John E. Schwarz and Thomas J. Volgy, "Above the Poverty Line—But Poor," *The Nation*, 15 February 1993, p. 191.

26. Robert D. Hershey, Jr., "Q & A: Mollie Orshansky, The Hand That Shaped America's Poverty Line as the Realistic Index," *New York Times*, 4 August 1989, p. A11.

27. Orshansky is quoted as saying, "If I write about the poor I don't need a good imagination—I have a good memory." William J. Eaton, "The Poverty Line," *New York Post Magazine*, 4 April 1970, p. 4.

28. U.S. Department of Health, Education, and Welfare, "The Measure of Poverty: Technical Paper III," in Oster, Lake, and Oksman, *The Definition and Measurement of Poverty, Vol. 1: A Review*, summary review paper, p. 7.

29. A fair market rent is defined by the U.S. Department of Housing and Urban Development as "decent, safe, and sanitary" housing of a "modest" nature. See Center for Social Welfare Policy and Law, *Living at the Bottom: An Analysis of AFDC Benefit Levels*, July 1993, Table 5, p. 29.

30. Robert Pear, "Auditors Want to Change Federal Poverty Definition," *New York Times*, 5 August 1994, p. A10.

31. Joel A. Devine and James D. Wright, *The Greatest of Evils: Urban Poverty and the American Underclass* (New York: Aldine de Gruyter, 1993), p. 15.

32. U.S. Bureau of the Census, *Current Population Reports*, Series P60-186RD, *Measuring the Effects of Benefits and Taxes on Income and Poverty: 1992*, pp. ix-x.

33. William O'Hare, Taynia Mann, Kathryn Porter, Robert Greenstein, *Real Life Poverty in America: Where the American Public Would Set the Poverty Line* (Washington, D.C.: Center on Budget and Policy Priorities, July 1990), p. 11.

34. While the basic formula for arriving at the poverty index has remained the same as it was when it was originally devised (three times the minimal food budget), certain other changes have been made in the way in which the formula is adjusted for different classes of people. While Orshansky's original formula called for adjusting the poverty level according to the sex of the family head, number of minors, and for farm families, these adjustments have since been dispensed with. In 1975 the Economy Food Plan was replaced by the Thrifty Food Plan, an updated plan designed to cost the same as the EFP. The 1977-1978 Nationwide Food Consumption Survey indicated that fewer than one in ten families spending an amount equal to the cost of the Thrifty Food Plan were able to purchase a diet that met recommended dietary allowances for all major nutrients. See Betty Peterkin and Richard L. Kerr, "Food Stamp Allotment and Diet of U.S. Households," *Family Economics Review*, Winter 1982.

35. Mollie Orshansky, "How Poverty is Measured," *Monthly Labor Review*, February 1969, p. 38; "Counting the Poor: Another Look at the Poverty Profile," *Social Security Bulletin*, October 1988, pp. 22-24; William J. Eaton, "The Poverty Line," p. 4.

36. Every year the Gallup organization asks a nationally representative sample of Americans what amount of income they would use as a poverty line for a family of four. The average that emerged from this survey in 1989 was 24

percent higher than the government's poverty line. When asked a related, but different question: "What is the smallest amount of money a family of four needs each week to get along in this community?" the survey respondents' answer was 73 percent higher than the then-current poverty line. See O'Hare, Mann, Porter, and Greenstein, *Real Life Poverty in America.*

37. Patricia Ruggles, *Drawing the Line: Alternative Poverty Measures and Their Implications for Public Policy* (Washington, D.C.: The Urban Institute Press, 1990).

38. U.S. Bureau of the Census, *Current Population Reports,* Series P60-188, *Income, Poverty and Valuation of Noncash Benefits: 1993* p. vii.

39. "Census Bureau Sued Over Homeless Count," *New York Times,* 11 October 1992, p. 37; Felicity Barringer, "U.S. Judge Upholds Population Count," *New York Times,* 14 April 1993, p. A14.

40. Sam Roberts, "Politics and Aid Could Shift in '90 Census Readjustment," *New York Times,* 21 August 1994, p. 50.

41. A 1976 study compared the aggregate of income reported to the Census Bureau against the aggregate estimates of income from Gross National Product (GNP) statistics. It found that the Census Bureau succeeded in counting 98.3 percent of wage and salary income, 91.1 percent of entrepreneurial income, but only 45 percent of property income. In comparison with other industrialized countries (with the exception of France), the United States was found to have the most inaccurate count of capital income. See M. Sawyer, "Income Distribution in OECD Countries," occasional paper, *OECD Economic Outlook* (Paris) July 1976, cited in Lars Osberg, *Economic Inequality in the United States* (New York: M.E. Sharpe, 1984), p. 25. A study comparing reports of money income reported to the Census Bureau with responses to income reported to the IRS for tax purposes found that the Census Bureau underreported property income by as much as 135 percent. See D.S. Radner, "An Example of the Use of Statistical Matching in the Estimation and Analysis of the Size Distribution of Income," *Review of Income and Wealth,* series 27 (3), September 1981, pp. 211-242, cited in Osberg, ibid.

42. U.S. Bureau of the Census, *Current Population Reports,* Series P60-185, *Poverty in the United States: 1992* (Washington, D.C.: U.S. Government Printing Office, 1993), Table C-1, p. C-2.

43. Other options that both the Census Bureau and academic researchers have considered are adjusting the income figures for the effect of taxes, capital gains, employee health benefits, and net return on home equity.

44. For detailed discussions of the complexities of adding in-kind government transfers to income calculations in determining poverty status, see U.S. Bureau of the Census, *Current Population Reports,* Series P60-188, *Income, Poverty and Noncash Valuation of Benefits: 1993,* pp. xvii-xxiv. See also Osberg, *Economic Inequality in the United States,* pp. 50-51; Benjamin I. Page, *Who Get's What From Government* (Berkeley, CA: University of California Press, 1983), pp. 206-7; Robert Greenstein, monograph, "Attempts to Dismiss the Census Poverty Data" (Washington, D.C.: Center on Budget and Policy Priorities, 28 September 1993); O'Hare, Mann, Porter, and Greenstein, *Real Life Poverty in America.*

45. Bill Kovach, "Federal Panel Considering Shift in the Definition of Who is Poor," *New York Times,* 7 April 1973, p. 36.

46. The Heritage Foundation, monograph, "How 'Poor' are America's Poor," 21 September 1990.

47. Greenstein, "Attempts to Dismiss the Census Poverty Data."

48. Bureau of the Census Current Population Reports, Series P60-186RD, *Measuring the Effect of Benefits and Taxes on Income and Poverty: 1992.*

49. Robert Pear, "A Proposed Definition of Poverty May Raise Number of U.S. Poor," *New York Times,* 30 April 1995, p. 1.

50. Norman Frumkin, *Tracking the Nation's Economy,* 2nd ed. (Armonk, N.Y.: M.E. Sharpe, 1992), p. 177.

51. The logic of economist A.W. Phillips's "Curve" theory is that declining unemployment leads to higher production costs as more outmoded and inefficient machinery is used and less-productive workers are employed. In addition, in a tight labor market, workers are freer to bid up wages and benefits when they know that if they are fired, they can easily get another job. More recently, the wage-rate component has been replaced by prices.

52. William Vickrey, "The Other Side of the Coin," acceptance paper delivered at the Frank E. Seidman Distinguished Award in Political Economy, Rhodes College, Memphis, Tennessee, 24 September 1992 (Memphis: P.K. Seidman Foundation, October 1992), p. 8.

53. Michael D. Yates, *Longer Hours, Fewer Jobs,* pp. 56-59.

54. Keith Bradsher, "Federal Reserve Raises Key Rates to Curb Growth," *New York Times,* 5 May 1994, p. 1.

55. Bryan Snyder, "Bad Medicine: Is the 'Cure' for Inflation Worth the Cost?," *Dollars and Sense* No. 194 (July/August 1994), pp. 11-12.

56. Louis Uchitelle, "Why America Won't Boom," *New York Times,* 12 June 1994, p. 1.

57. Louis Uchitelle, "Growth of Jobs May be Casualty in Inflation Fight," *New York Times,* 24 April 1994, p. 1.

58. Households in the Census Bureau survey are interviewed for four consecutive months, leave the sample for the next eight months, and then come back into the sample for four more consecutive months before leaving the sample for good. In the household's first and fifth months, interviews are conducted in person at the respondents' homes. In the remaining months, interviews are typically done over the telephone. Respondents in households without a telephone, as well as those with language or hearing difficulties, are interviewed in person each month. Interviews are conducted on the same day each month and most questions relate to activity in the prior week, known as the reference week. See U.S. Department of Labor Bureau of Labor Statistics, "Questions and Answers on the Redesign of the Current Population Survey" (November 1993).

59. Beginning in 1994, the unemployment rate and all other labor market data reflected the results of a major redesign, meant to capture changes that had been occurring in the economy over the last two decades. While this revision represents an improvement over the way the Census Bureau conducted its previous surveys, the unemployment rate, like the poverty rate, still hides as much as it reveals.

60. Yates, *Longer Hours, Fewer Jobs,* p. 62.

61. See fact sheet: "Welfare Reform: Where Are the Jobs?," National Jobs for All Coalition, 475 Riverside Drive, New York, NY 10115.
62. Frumkin, *Tracking America's Economy*, p. 18.

CHAPTER 3: FROM THEORY TO POLICY

1. For a historical summary of the changing conceptions of the poor, see Michael B. Katz, *The Undeserving Poor: From the War on Poverty to the War on Welfare* (New York: Pantheon Books, 1989).
2. For a history of the development of poor relief, see Michael B. Katz, *In the Shadow of the Poorhouse: A Social History of Welfare in America* (New York: Basic Books/HarperCollins, 1986).
3. Katz, *The Undeserving Poor*, p. 14.
4. Ibid., p. 15.
5. Ibid., pp. 70-123.
6. For accounts of the change in focus of the civil rights leadership, see Martin Luther King, Jr., *Where Do We Go From Here: Chaos or Community?* (New York: Harper & Row, 1967); C.T. Vivian, *Black Power and the American Myth* (Philadelphia: Fortress Press, 1970).
7. *Report of the National Advisory Commission on Civil Disorders* (New York: The New York Times Co./Bantam Books, 1968), p. 1.
8. Oscar Lewis, *La Vida: A Puerto Rican Family in the Culture of Poverty—San Juan and New York* (New York: Vintage Books/Random House, 1965); Daniel Patrick Moynihan, *The Negro Family: The Case for National Action* (Washington, D.C.: Office of Policy Planning and Research, United States Department of Labor, March 1965); Edward C. Banfield, *The Unheavenly City: The Nature and Future of our Urban Crisis* (Boston: Little Brown and Co., 1970); and *The Unheavenly City Revisited* (Boston: Little Brown and Co., 1974). The second book is a thorough revision and expansion of the original.
9. Lewis, pp. xlii-lii.
10. Ibid., p. xliii.
11. Ibid., p. xlviii.
12. Ibid., p. xii.
13. The full report and the controversy that surrounded it can be found in Lee Rainwater and William L. Yancey, *The Moynihan Report and the Politics of Controversy* (Cambridge, MA: The M.I.T. Press, 1967).
14. Ibid., p. 26.
15. Moynihan, p. 5. For more on Moynihan's emphasis on family structure as the root cause of poverty, see Rainwater and Yancey, pp. 20, 22.
16. Moynihan, pp. 28-29.
17. Herbert Gutman, *The Black Family in Slavery and Freedom, 1750-1925* (New York: Vintage Books/Random House, 1976). Gutman's work, based on extensive Freedman's Bureau and other literary records, was stimulated by the controversy that had surrounded the Moynihan report. In it he demonstrated that Moynihan had underestimated the adaptive capacities of the enslaved and their descendents whose families remained remarkably intact at least through the 1920s.

18. Carol Stack, *All Our Kin: Strategies for Survival in a Black Community* (New York: Harper & Row, 1974).

19. James Farmer, "The Core of It," *Amsterdam News* (New York), 18 December 1985. Reprinted in Rainwater and Yancey, p. 410.

20. Banfield, *The Unheavenly City Revisited*, p. 142.

21. Ibid., p. 143.

22. Ibid., p. 54.

23. Ibid., p. 57.

24. George Gilder, *Wealth and Poverty* (New York: Basic Books, 1981).

25. Ibid., p. 73.

26. Ibid., p. 70.

27. Ibid., p. 116.

28. Ibid., p. 111.

29. Ibid., p. 117.

30. Ibid., p. 126.

31. Ibid., p. 67.

32. Charles Murray, *Losing Ground: American Social Policy, 1950-1980* (New York: Basic Books, 1984).

33. Murray, *Losing Ground*, pp. 233-34.

34. For a summary of the critique of Murray's work, see Katz, (1989), pp. 153-56; Theodore R. Marmor, Jerry L. Mashaw, and Philip L. Harvey, *America's Misunderstood Welfare State: Persistent Myths, Enduring Realities* (New York: Basic Books, 1990), pp. 104-14. See also William E. Schmidt, "Study Links Male Unemployment and Single Mothers in Chicago," *New York Times*, 15 January 1989, p. 16, for an account of a study that refutes Murray's argument that providing money to poor people discourages seeking and holding jobs and family stability.

35. Katz, *The Undeserving Poor*, p. 55.

36. Ibid., p. 156.

37. Lawrence M. Mead, *Beyond Entitlement: The Social Obligations of Citizenship* (New York: The Free Press, 1986), p. ix.

38. Ibid., p. 1.

39. Ibid., pp. 68-69.

40. Ibid., p. 84.

41. Richard Hofstadter, *Social Darwinism in American Thought* (Boston: Beacon Press, 1955).

42. Jason DeParle, "Daring Research or 'Social Science Pornography'? Charles Murray," *New York Times Magazine*, 9 October 1994, p. 50.

43. Auletta's conception of the underclass is fully described in Ken Auletta, *The Underclass* (New York: Vintage Books/Random House, 1982).

44. Ibid., pp. 43-44.

45. See, for examples: Herbert J. Gans, "The Dangers of the Underclass: Its Harmfulness as a Planning Concept," Working Paper #4, Russell Sage Foundation (January 1990); Walter W. Stafford and Joyce Ladner, "Political Dimensions of the Underclass Concept," in *Sociology and Critical American Issues* (Newbury Park, CA: Sage Publications, 1991), pp. 138-55.

46. Jacqueline Jones, *The Dispossessed: America's Underclasses From the Civil War to the Present* (New York: Basic Books, 1992).

47. William Julius Wilson, *The Truly Disadvantaged: The Inner City, the Underclass, and Public Policy* (Chicago: University of Chicago Press, 1987).

48. Christopher Jencks, *Rethinking Social Policy: Race, Poverty, and the Underclass* (Cambridge, MA: Harvard University Press, 1992), p. 141.

49. William Julius Wilson and Loic Wacquant, "Poverty, Joblessness and the Inner City," in Phoebe H. Cottingham and David T. Ellwood, eds., *Welfare Policy for the 1990s* (Cambridge, MA: Harvard University Press, 1989), p. 78.

50. Ibid., p. 86, 88.

51. Isabel Wilkerson, "How Milwaukee Has Thrived While Leaving Blacks Behind," *New York Times*, 19 March 1991, p. 1.

52. Wilson and Wacquant, p. 95.

53. Jencks, pp. 136-37.

54. Wilson and Wacquant, p. 102.

55. Robert B. Reich, *The Work of Nations: Preparing Ourselves for 21st Century Capitalism* (New York: Vintage Books, 1992), pp. 172-73.

56. Ibid., p. 177.

57. Ibid., pp. 197-98.

58. Ibid., pp. 202-3.

59. Ibid., pp. 245-50.

60. Ibid., pp. 311-12.

61. See: Mimi Abramovitz, *Regulating the Lives of Women: Social Welfare Policy From Colonial Times to the Present* (Boston: South End Press, 1988); Teresa Amott, *Caught in the Crisis: Women and the U.S. Economy Today* (New York: Monthly Review Press, 1993); Amott and Julie Matthaei, *Race, Gender, and Work: A Multicultural Economic History of Women in the United States* (Boston: South End Press, 1991); Lourdes Beneria and Shelley Feldman, eds., *Unequal Burden: Economic Crises, Persistent Poverty, and Women's Work* (Boulder, CO: Westview Press, 1992); Goldberg and Kremen, eds., *The Feminization of Poverty*; Diana Pearce, "Welfare is Not *For* Women: Why the War on Poverty Cannot Conquer the Feminization of Poverty," in Linda Gordon, ed., *Women, the State and Welfare* (Madison: University of Wisconsin Press, 1990), pp. 265-79; and Ruth Sidel, *Women and Children Last: The Plight of Poor Women in Affluent America* (New York: Penguin Books, 1986). For many papers on women's economic and political status, see the works put out by Heidi Hartmann and Roberta Spalter-Roth at the Institute for Women's Policy Research, Washington, D.C.

62. Julianne Malveaux, "The Economic Interests of Black and White Women: Are They Similar?," *Review of Black Political Economy*, Summer 1985, pp. 5-27.

63. Sheila D. Collins, Gertrude Schaffner Goldberg and Helen Lachs Ginsburg, *Jobs for All: A Plan for the Revitalization of America* (New York: The Apex Press, 1994), pp. 61-64.

65. Jesse Jackson; Manning Marable, Director of the Institute for African Americans Studies at Columbia University, and Cornel West, professor of African American Studies at Harvard, take this approach. See Sheila D. Collins, *The Rainbow Challenge: The Jackson Campaign and the Future of U.S. Politics* (New York: Monthly Review Press, 1987); Manning Marable, "History and Black Consciousness: The Political Culture of Black America," *Monthly Review* 47,

No. 3 (July/August 1995): 71-88; and Cornel West, *Race Matters* (Boston: Beacon Press, 1994).

66. See Helen Ginsburg, *Full Employment and Public Policy: The United States and Sweden* (Lexington, MA: Lexington Books/D.C. Heath & Co., 1983); and Gary Mucciaroni, *The Political Failure of Employment Policy, 1945-1982* (Pittsburgh: University of Pittsburgh Press, 1990), pp. 224-54.

CHAPTER 4: FROM POLICY TO PRACTICE

1. Timothy M. Smeeding and Lee Rainwater, "Cross-National Trends in Income, Poverty and Dependency: The Evidence for Young Adults in the Eighties," *The Luxembourg Income Study*, Working Paper #67. Prepared for the Joint Center for Policy Studies Conference on Poverty and Social Marginality, Washington, D.C., September 20-21, 1991.

2. Ibid., pp. 29-37.

3. Charles I. Schottland, "Introduction," in Charles I. Schottland, ed. *The Welfare State* (New York: Harper & Row, 1967), pp. 9-45.

4. For a history of this concept, see William Appleman Williams, *Empire as a Way of Life* (New York: Oxford University Press, 1980).

5. Theodore R. Marmor, Jerry L. Mashaw, and Philip L. Harvey, *America's Misunderstood Welfare State* (New York: Basic Books, 1990), p. 4.

6. For an extensive critique of individualism and its impact on American life and institutions, see Robert N. Bellah, Richard Madsen, William M. Sullivan, Ann Swidler, and Steven M. Tipton, *The Good Society* (New York: Random House, 1991).

7. Marmor, Mashaw, and Harvey, pp. 4-6.

8. James Madison, Federalist Paper No. 10 in Alexander Hamilton, James Madison, John Jay, *The Federalist Papers* (New York: New American Library, 1961), pp. 77-84.

9. Frances Fox Piven and Richard A. Cloward, *Why Americans Don't Vote* (New York: Pantheon Books, 1988), pp. 48-69.

10. Francis Fox Piven and Richard A. Cloward, *Regulating the Poor: The Functions of Public Welfare*, 2nd ed. (New York: Random House, 1993), p. 77.

11. Michael B. Katz, *In the Shadow of the Poorhouse: A Social History of Welfare in America* (New York: Basic Books, 1986), p. 207.

12. Even before 1933, there had been broad agreement that spending on public projects should be increased during economic downturns, but this was largely seen as a function of local government. See Margaret Weir, *Politics and Jobs: The Boundaries of Employment Policy in the United States* (Princeton: Princeton University Press, 1992), p. 29.

13. Ibid., pp. 34-35.

14. Anthony J. Badger, *The New Deal: The Depression Years, 1933-1940* (New York: Hill and Wang, 1989), pp. 108-11.

15. In addition to deficit spending, Sweden's early emergence from the Depression is attributed to, among other things, a low interest-rate policy, the stabilization of farm prices, the modernization of industry, and depreciation of the kronor. See Helen Ginsburg, *Full Employment and Public Policy: The*

United States and Sweden (Lexington, MA: Lexington Books/D.C. Heath & Co., 1983), pp. 111-12; and Gary Mucciaroni, *The Political Failure of Full Employment Policy, 1945-1982* (Pittsburgh: University of Pittsburgh Press, 1992), pp. 224-54.

16. For histories of the New Deal programs, see Nancy E. Rose, *Put to Work: Relief Programs in the Great Depression* (New York: Monthly Review Press, 1994); and Badger, *The New Deal*.

17. Katz, *In the Shadow of the Poorhouse*, p. 225.

18. Rose, pp. 26, 47.

19. Piven & Cloward, *Regulating the Poor*, p. 73.

20. Ibid., pp. 88-89.

21. Rose, pp. 26-27.

22. Ibid., pp. 32-33.

23. Piven and Cloward, *Regulating the Poor*, p. 76.

24. Rose, p. 37.

25. Piven & Cloward, *Regulating the Poor*, pp. 84-85.

26. Rose, pp. 80-88.

27. American Social History Project, *Who Built America? Working People and the Nation's Economy, Politics, Culture and Society*, Vol. 2 (New York: Pantheon Books, 1992), p. 371.

28. The Social Security Act of 1935 provided benefits only to retired workers themselves, but in 1939 the first of numerous extensions to the system provided benefits for survivors and dependents.

29. Gertrude S. Goldberg, "The Revision of Societal Knowledge in the Great Depression," unpublished paper, Summer 1968.

30. Senator Patrick Harrison's remarks were quoted in the *New York Times*, 11 June 1935, cited in Goldberg, p. 15.

31. Roosevelt's remarks cited in Carl P. Chelf, *Controversial Issues in Social Welfare Policy: Government and the Pursuit of Happiness*, Vol. 3 (Newbury Park, CA: Sage Publications, 1992), p. 33.

32. The original plan for Social Security had called for social insurance to be financed out of general revenues (as much of the European welfare state is), but the opposition of Republicans and Southern Democrats in Congress forced the government to turn to the more regressive payroll tax.

33. A 1987 study by the Social Security Administration revealed that 80 percent of the elderly had no other sources of income but Social Security. See R.F. Pollack, "The Elderly's Wealth is Exaggerated," in D. Bender and B. Leone, eds., *The Elderly: Opposing Viewpoints* (San Diego: Greenhaven Press, 1990), pp. 79-84, cited in Chelf, p. 34.

34. Rose, pp. 96-99; Piven and Cloward, *Regulating the Poor*, pp. 95-100.

35. American Social History Project, p. 375; Ginsburg, p. 11; Rose, pp. 104-7.

36. The initial version of the Social Security Act would have provided public employment for anyone who had exhausted their unemployment compensation as well as to "able-bodied" workers not covered by unemployment insurance. See Rose, p. 92.

37. Ibid., pp. 98-101.

38. Piven and Cloward, *Regulating the Poor*, p. 98.

39. This is the thesis of Piven and Cloward's *Regulating the Poor*.

40. Katz, *In the Shadow of the Poorhouse*, p. 235.

41. See Sar A. Levitan and Clifford M. Johnson, *Beyond the Safety Net: Reviving the Promise of Opportunity in America* (Cambridge, MA: Ballinger Publishing Co., 1984), pp. 4-5.

42. Excerpted from Franklin Delano Roosevelt, eleventh annual State of the Union Address, January 11, 1944, in Fred L. Israel, ed., *The State of the Union Messages of the President, 1790-1966*, Vol. 3 (New York: Chelsea House, Robert Hector Publishers, 1966), p. 2881.

43. See Stephen Kemp Bailey, *Congress Makes a Law* (New York: Vintage Books, 1960). See also Ginsburg, pp. 13-17.

44. Katz, *The Undeserving Poor*, pp. 89-90.

45. Mucciaroni, *The Political Failure of Full Employment Policy*, pp. 25-30.

46. Katz, *In the Shadow of the Poorhouse*, p. 255-56.

47. Katz, *The Undeserving Poor*, p. 95.

48. Piven and Cloward, *Regulating the Poor*, pp. 256-63.

49. Ibid., pp. 256-76. See also Katz, *The Undeserving Poor*, pp. 85-88.

50. As poverty programs in the South made thousands of jobs available to civil rights workers, the programs became deeply entwined with the civil rights movement and faced opposition from segregationist forces. See Piven and Cloward, *Regulating the Poor*, p. 281.

51. Piven, "The Great Society," p. 311, cited in Katz, *The Undeserving Poor*, p. 98.

52. John C. Donovan, *The Politics of Poverty* (New York: Pegasus, 1967), p. 55.

53. Jill Quadragno, *The Color of Welfare: How Racism Undermined the War on Poverty* (New York: Oxford University Press, 1994), p. 20, and Sheila D. Collins, *The Rainbow Challenge* (New York: Monthly Review Press, 1987), pp. 67-70.

54. Quadragno, p. 155.

55. Ibid., pp. 50-51.

56. Piven and Cloward, *Regulating the Poor*, p. 463.

57. Quadragno, p. 175.

58. Katz, *In the Shadow of the Poorhouse*, p. 257.

59. Katz, *The Undeserving Poor*, pp. 112-13.

60. See the arguments for their case in the appendix to *Regulating the Poor*, pp. 461-66.

61. Katz, *The Undeserving Poor*, p. 114.

62. Levitan and Johnson, p. 2.

63. Evaluations of the political and administrative difficulties of CETA are found in Paul Bullock, *CETA at the Crossroads: Employment Policy and Politics* (Los Angeles: Institute of Industrial Relations, University of California, Los Angeles); Ginsburg, *Full Employment and Public Policy*, pp. 51-55; and Mucciaroni, *The Political Failure of Employment Policy*, pp. 158-92.

64. Collins, *The Rainbow Challenge*, pp. 52-59.

65. Thomas Byrne Edsall, *The New Politics of Inequality* (New York: W.W. Norton, 1984), p. 107.

66. For detailed accounts of the demise of New Deal liberalism and the rise of a resurgent conservatism, see Edsall, *The New Politics of Inequality*; William Grieder, *Who Will Tell the People: The Betrayal of Democracy* (New York: Simon & Schuster, 1992); and Kevin Phillips, *The Politics of Rich and Poor: Wealth and*

the American Electorate in the Reagan Aftermath (New York: HarperPerennial, 1990), pp. 32-36.

67. See Robert Sherrill,"S & Ls, Big Banks and Other Triumphs of Capitalism," *The Nation*, 19 November 1990, p. 592. Under Carter, a conservative Democratic congress passed the first of a series of tax reforms (1978) that cut in half the capital gains tax (the tax that overwhelmingly hits the rich), lowered the corporate tax rate, and made the temporary investment-tax credit for business permanent. See Grieder, *Who Will Tell the People*, p. 89.

68. For a description of the way in which the religious right reshaped the Republican Party, see Haynes Johnson, *Sleepwalking Through History: America in the Reagan Years* (New York: W.W. Norton, 1991), pp. 193-214.

69. See Collins, Chapter 2, pp. 51-82.

70. See "Part 2: The New Right and the American Way," *Spotlight*, October 1980, p. 3; Barbara Ehrenreich, "The New Right Attack on Social Welfare," in Fred Block, Richard A. Cloward, Barbara Ehrenreich, and Frances Fox Piven, *The Mean Season: The Attack on the Welfare State* (New York: Pantheon Books, 1987), pp. 161-95.

71. For critiques of the new right's economic arguments for dismantling the welfare state, see Block, Cloward, Ehrenreich, and Piven; Robert Kuttner, *The Economic Illusion: False Choices Between Prosperity and Social Justice* (New York: Houghton Mifflin, 1984); Levitan and Johnson, pp. 55-110.

72. Evelyn Z. Brodkin, "The War Against Welfare," *Dissent*, Spring 1995, pp. 211-20.

73. A detailed history of the new right's political, financial, and intellectual connections can be found in Russ Bellant, *The Coors Connection: how Coors Family Philanthropy Undermines Democratic Pluralism* (Boston: South End Press, 1991) and Alan Crawford, *Thunder on the Right* (New York: Pantheon, 1980).

74. Grieder, *Who Will Tell the People?*, p. 39.

75. Newt Gingrich, remarks at the Young Republican Leadership Conference, Washington, D.C., March 19, 1992, quoted in Amy D. Bernstein and Peter W. Bernstein, eds., *Quotations from Speaker Newt: The Little Red, White and Blue Book of the Republican Revolution* (New York: Workman Publishing, 1995), p. 28.

76. Katz, *In the Shadow of the Poorhouse*, pp. 280-83; and Robert Fitch, *The Assassination of New York* (London: Verso, 1993).

77. Phillips, *The Politics of Rich and Poor*, pp. 76-115.

78. For a history of how "supply side" came to dominate the economic thinking of Reagan officials, see Johnson, *Sleepwalking Through History*, pp. 97-115.

79. Ibid., p. 98.

80. Ibid., p. 111.

81. William Grieder, "The Education of David Stockman," *Atlantic Monthly*, December 1981, p. 47.

82. Ibid., p. 27.

83. David Stockman, quoted in Johnson, p. 109.

84. Conservative insiders were clear about the political use of block grants. A member of a conservative foundation who attended a Conservative Caucus briefing in June 1981 noted: "It was emphasized how extremely important it is for this legislation [block grants] to be passed. The 'block grant system'

is the major strategy conceived in order to pull the rug out from under the liberals and leave them completely powerless or 'no longer any reason to exist.'" Memo to members of the foundation community, in author's possession.

85. Greider, "The Education of David Stockman," p. 35.
86. Katz, *In the Shadow of the Poorhouse*, p. 286.
87. Phillips, p. 76.
88. Greider, "The Education of David Stockman," p. 46. In a subsequent attempt to recover lost tax revenue, Congress raised the highest rate to 31 percent and then to 36 percent under Clinton; but they never returned to the progressive rate structure that had prevailed in earlier decades.
89. Katz, *In the Shadow of the Poorhouse*, p. 288.
90. Citizens for Tax Justice, *Corporate Income Taxes in the Reagan Years* (Washington, D.C.: Citizens for Tax Justice, 1984).
91. Citizens for Tax Justice, *Inequality and the Federal Budget Deficit* (Washington, D.C.: Citizens for Tax Justice, September 1991), p. 12.
92. Phillips, p. 78.
93. John Allen Poulos, "The S & L Tab," *New York Times*, 28 June 1991, p. A25; Robert Sherrill, p. 589.
94. Johnson, p. 111.

CHAPTER 5: HOW POVERTY WON THE WAR

1. See Paul Leonard and Robert Greenstein, *Life Under the Spending Caps: The Clinton Fiscal Year 1995 Budget* (Washington, D.C.: Center on Budget and Policy Priorities, April 1994). Under both the 1990 and 1993 budget acts, any action by Congress to increase an entitlement program or cut taxes would have to be "paid for" through an offsetting entitlement reduction or tax increase.
2. Pollsters found that only one-sixth of the minority of registered voters who had voted in November regarded the outcome as "an affirmation of the Republican agenda" and an overwhelming majority had never even heard of the Contract. Most of the voters polled opposed defense increases, and 61 percent of them said that "spending for domestic programs should be increased." See Noam Chomsky, "Rollback Part I," *Z Magazine*, January 1995, p. 20.
3. David E. Sanger, "Republicans Want to Renew Vision of Reagan (Then Redo His Math)," *New Yoek Times*, 15 January 1995, p. A18.
4. The estimated loss to state and local governments of federal cutbacks was done by Fiscal Planning Services for the Center on Budget and Policy Priorities using Congressional Budget Office data published on January 5, 1995. The estimate was made using currently projected baselines for each year from 1996 to 2002 and was based on the assumption of a balanced budget by 2002, enactment of deep tax cuts, and the protection of Social Security and defense spending from budget cuts. See Center on Budget and Policy Priorities (Washington, D.C.), *Holding the Bag: The Effect on State and*

Local Governments of the Emerging Fiscal Agenda in the 104th Congress, January 31, 1995.

5. Center on Social Welfare Policy and Law (New York), *Jobless, Penniless, Often Homeless: State General Assistance Cuts Leave 'Employable' Struggling for Survival*, Publication No. 805, February 1994.

6. "Connecticut Lawmakers Approve Strict New Welfare Rules," *New York Times*, 4 June 1995, p. 4.

7. Jonathan Rabinovitz, "Court Allows Welfare Cuts in Connecticut," *New York Times*, 20 June 1995, p. B1.

8. Alison Mitchell, "In New York, the Dying Days of Expansive Government," *New York Times*, 8 May 1995, p. 1.

9. Pamela Sebastian, "Corporate Giving Had Lower Showing in 1994," *Wall Street Journal*, 25 May 1995, p. A22.

10. Gary D. Bass, "Gingrich's 'Contract' Would Devastate Charities," *The Chronicle of Philanthropy*, 13 December 1994, pp. 42-43.

11. Sebastian, "Corporate Giving."

12. Robin Toner, "Tax Cut Edges Out Deficit as G.O.P.'s Guiding Tenet," *New York Times*, 3 April 1995, p. 1.

13. Center on Budget and Policy Priorities (Washington, D.C.), *The New Fiscal Agenda: What Will it Mean and How Will it be Accomplished?*, January 1995, p. 5.

14. David E. Rosenbaum, "Chairman Proposes Redefining Tax Code," *New York Times*, 7 June 1995, p. A22.

15. See Edward S. Herman and Noam Chomsky, *Manufacturing Consent: The Political Economy of the Mass Media* (New York: Pantheon, 1988).

16. William Greider, *Who Will Tell the People: The Betrayal of American Democracy* (New York: Simon & Schuster, 1992). See also Kevin Phillips, *Arrogant Capital: Washington, Wall Street and the Frustration of American Politics* (Boston: Little Brown & Co., 1994).

17. For detailed analyses of the globalization process, see Samir Amin, "Fifth Years is Enough," *Monthly Review* 46, No. 11 (April 1995): 8-50, and *Maldevelopment: Anatomy of a Global Failure* (London: United Nations University Press, 1990); Richard J. Barnet and John Cavanagh, *Global Dreams: Imperial Corporations and the New World Order* (New York: Simon & Schuster, 1994); Stephen Gill and David Law, *The Global Political Economy: Perspectives, Problems and Politics* (Baltimore: The Johns Hopkins University Press, 1988); Arthur MacEwen, *Debt and Disorder: International Economic Instability and U.S. Imperial Decline* (New York: Monthly Review Press, 1990); Arthur MacEwen and William K. Tabb, eds., *Instability and Change in the World Economy* (New York: Monthly Review Press, 1989); and Harry Magdoff, *Globalization: To What End?* (New York: Monthly Review Press, 1992).

18. International Labor Organization (Geneva), *World Employment Report 1995*, pp. 194-95.

19. Kevin Phillips, *Arrogant Capital*, p. 86.

20. *The Economist*, 27 April 1991, quoted in Magdoff, *Globalization: To What End?*, p. 19.

21. International Labor Organization, *World Employment Report 1995*; and Mihaly Simai, ed., *Global Employment: An International Investigation into the*

Future of Work, Vol. 1 (London: United Nations University World Institute for Development Economics Research/Zed Books, 1995).

22. United Nations Department of Economic and Social Information and Policy Analysis, *World Economic and Social Survey 1994* (New York: United Nations, 1994), pp. 2-3.

23. Ibid.; International Labor Organization, *World Employment Report 1995*.

24. Craig R. Whitney, "Jobless Legions Rattle Europe's Welfare States," *New York Times*, 14 June 1995, p. A3.

25. Dana Milibank, "Unlike Rest of Europe, Britain is Creating Jobs, But They Pay Poorly," *Wall Street Journal*, 28 March 1994, p. 1. Britain's policy, much like ours, has resulted in the weakening of workers' rights, the elimination of the minimum wage, and declining wages and benefits.

26. Barnet and Cavanagh, *Global Dreams*, p. 15.

27. "And the Correct Answer Is—," *Public Citizen*, February 1995.

28. David E. Sanger, "Do Fickle Markets Now Make Policy?" *New York Times*, 19 March 1995, p. D3.

29. International Labor Organization, *World Employment Report 1995*, pp. 196-97.

30. Keith Bradsher, "Doubts Voiced by Greenspan on a Rate Cut," *New York Times*, 21 June 1995, p. 1. For an explanation of the Mexican crisis and the role of foreign investors in bringing it about, see Doug Henwood, "The Contract With Mexico," *Left Business Observer*, No. 68, 14 March 1995; and James M. Sypher, "NAFTA Shock: Mexico's Free Market Meltdown," *Dollars and Sense*, No. 198, March/April 1995.

31. William S. Vickrey, "The Other Side of the Coin," acceptance paper in response to the Frank E. Seidman DIstinguished Award in Political Economy, Rhodes College, Memphis, TN (24 September 1992), p. 9.

32. Nathaniel C. Nash, "U.S. Savings and Deficit Key to Dollar, German Says," *New York Times*, 8 May 1995, p. 1.

33. Thomas L. Friedman, "Cold War Agency Looks at Problems Back Home," *New York Times*, 26 June 1994, p. 1.

34. David Moberg, "The Great Divide," *In These Times*, 12 June 1995, p. 35.

35. Nathaniel C. Nash, "Paris Markets Wary on Plan for Economy," 30 May 1995, p. D1.

36. Phillip Frazer and Jeremy Weintraub, "An American Ruling Class?" *The Washington Spectator* 19, No. 7 (1 April 1993):2-3.

37. Jeff Gerth and Stephen Labaton, "The Local Forces That Helped Shape Gingrich as a Foe of Regulation," *New York Times*, 12 February 1995, p. 22.

38. Associated Press Online, 21 June 1995.

39. George Miller, "Authors of the Law," *New York Times*, 24 May 1995, p. A21.

40. Stephen Engelberg, "100 Days of Dreams Come True for Lobbyists in Congress," *New York Times*, 14 April 1995, p. A12.

41. Walter Russell Mead, "Forward to the Past," *New York Times Magazine*, 4 June 1995, p. 49.

42. See, for example, Harvey Brenner, *Estimating the Costs of National Economic Policy: Implications for Mental and Physical Health and Aggression*, study prepared for Joint Economic Commission of Congress (Washington, D.C.: U.S. Congress, 94th Congress, 2nd Session); Arloc Sherman, *Wasting*

America's Future: The Children's Defense Fund Report on the Costs of Child Poverty (Boston: Beacon Press, 1994); United Nations Department of Economic and Social Information and Policy Analysis, *World Economic and Social Survey, 1994* (New York: United Nations, 1994); the International Labor Organization's *World Employment Report*; and Andrew Glyn and David Miliband, *Paying for Inequality: The Economic Cost of Social Injustice* (London: IPPR/Rivers Oram Press, 1994).

43. This list would include the Economic Policy Institute, the Center on Budget and Policy Priorities, the Children's Defense Fund, the Center on Social Welfare Policy and Law, the Institute for Women's Policy Research, the Institute for Research in African American Studies, and the Interuniversity Center for Latino Research.

44. Timothy Canova, Sheila D. Collins, Helen Lachs Ginsburg, Gertrude Schaffner Goldberg, Sumner Rosen, and June Zaccone, "A Growth Agenda That Works," unpublished draft of a working paper of the National Jobs for All Coalition, June 1995, p. 23.

45. Sam Pizzagati, *The Minimum Wage: A Common Sense Prescription for Revitalizing America* (New York: The Apex Press, 1994). See also Bryan Snyder, "A Maximum Wage: How Much is Enough?," *Dollars and Sense*, July/August 1995, p. 30.

46. Edward N. Wolff, *Top Heavy: A Study of the Increasing Inequality of Wealth in America* (New York: The Twentieth Century Fund Press, 1995), pp. 51-57.

47. Bob Becker, "CDBG Abuse: Stop Using Our Taxes to Steal Our Jobs!" *Federation for Industrial Retention and Renewal News*, Vol. 7, No. 1 (Spring 1995): 18.

48. Jim Benn, "The Crisis, the Cities and Comprehensive Strategy," *Federation for Industrial Retention and Renewal News*, Vol. 7, No. 1: 2.

INDEX